VOLKSWAGEN GOLF GTI

THE ENTHUSIAST'S COMPANION

EDITOR: RAY HUTTON

MRP

MOTOR RACING PUBLICATIONS LTD
Unit 6, The Pilton Estate, 46 Pitlake, Croydon CR0 3RY, England.

ISBN 0 947981 05 5
First published 1985

Photosetting by Zee Creative Ltd., London SW16
Printed in Great Britain by Netherwood, Dalton & Co. Ltd.,
Bradley Mills, Huddersfield, West Yorkshire

For GTI enthusiasts only

This, we believe, is something new in motoring book publishing.

It is not about a 'classic' in the usually accepted sense of a 15-20 years old sports car — though there is no doubt that the Golf GTI is a classic of its kind. It is not a 'marque history' in the familiar mould, though the background to the GTI is described in detail for the first time. Neither is it a do-it-yourself workshop manual, though it is full of information and advice on owning and running a GTI.

We have brought together information, pictures and, most importantly, well-known specialist authors, to produce a book which gets beneath the fashionable skin of this 1980s cult car. Owners and would-be GTI owners will be informed, intrigued and delighted by what is within. It is a book to share the enjoyment of their chosen car: The Enthusiast's Companion.

CONTENTS

Inventing the Hot Hatch

How the GTI evolved and the development of the model that set a new class of sporting car

Sisters under the skin — the Golf and Scirocco GTIs went on sale simultaneously in 1976, sharing the same chassis set-up and the 1,588cc fuel-injected engine. Scirocco's lower-drag coupe body meant that its performance was slightly superior but the Golf GTI was to become the big seller.

Here we have something very unusual in the world of mass-production vehicles: an engineer's car.

In the early 1970s, when the Volkswagen Golf was under development, the 'hot hatch' didn't exist. There had been Mini-Coopers and fast versions of bigger saloons, but the motor industry's marketing experts saw the emerging trend to hatchbacks as a new generation of sensible, practical, small cars for the family motorist. If he or she wanted to go fast, there were sports cars or sports coupes.

Herbert Schuster, now Volkswagen's divisional manager of vehicle testing, recalls that the first ideas for a high-performance Golf were developed in March

1973 by an enthusiastic group of engineers working on the model's prototype, code-numbered EA337. 'It all started with just one car, and it was purely a private idea. Only the engineers — not the managers, and certainly not the sales department — were involved.'

Given the speed with which the mainstream Golf had to be brought to production, the 'Sport Golf' as the engineers called it, had to become an 'evenings and weekends' project, developed more-or-less secretly outside normal working hours. It was not until 1974, after the Golf had been launched, that the idea was even shown to Professor Fiala, the research and development chief, or the sales and marketing management. Then there was polite interest, but no more than that — the sales people were against it because they could not see a market for a sporting Golf.

Ten years later the GTI is produced at over 200 a day at the Wolfsburg factory and accounts for 12 per cent of European Golf production. A car of similar specification and character with the same name is made by Volkswagen's North American subsidiary. The GTI has won awards on both sides of the Atlantic and epitomizes the new breed of 'family sports cars'. Its formula and even its title have been copied by Volkswagen's rivals.

The engineers invented it, so this isn't a stripes-and-spoilers special that depends on publicity 'hype' or a loose association with a completely different competition car. Strength in engineering has been a major factor in Germany's high reputation in the modern motoring world. Volkswagen's 'New Generation' is part of that. Its evolution was an agonizing business, made complex by industrial and personal events and an underlying feeling held by many — perhaps including those who could not see a market for a sporting Golf, who knows? — that the best-selling Beetle was irreplaceable.

In the extraordinary series of events that led to the Golf — and ultimately the GTI — the basic engine had been laid down for an entirely different car and there was even a tenuous link with Mercedes-Benz engineering. Had things been different, the Golf might have had its engine in the middle driving the rear wheels, following the idea of the VW-Porsche sports cars sold in the early 1970s. The original Volkswagen — the Beetle — was the brainchild of the original Dr Porsche, so let's go back to the roots of the VW idea to see why and how they came to have the world's all-time best-selling car and so much trouble deciding where to go from there.

Ferdinand Porsche had already built a glittering reputation as a designer before he set up his own studios in the 1930s. Prototypes designed for other concerns led to Dr Porsche discussing a new 'people's car' project with the German Chancellor, Adolf Hitler. Out of this came a commission to design a new KdF car, for which an entirely new factory at Wolfsburg, east of Hannover, was to be built. If the Second World War had not intervened, mass production of the Beetle would have begun by the end of 1939. The dislocation, and the

Volkswagen success stories — replacing the Beetle, the world's all-time best-seller, was an agonizing business with a number of false starts but the Golf rang the bell and by the time the Mark 2 (right) appeared, had been European sales leader. The GTI accounts for some 12% of the 2,000-a-day Wolfsburg Golf production.

devastation, of war meant that first deliveries were made in 1945, with the factory under British Army direction. The basic layout of the Beetle — a car with a rear-mounted, air-cooled engine and all-independent suspension — persisted on all VWs produced in the next 25 years, and the huge expansion in production and sales was to the credit of Heinz Nordhoff. Beetle sales eventually passed the legendary Model T Ford's 15 million total in 1972 — but the same all-powerful executive steadfastly refused to commission any new models which did not stay faithful to the same layout. VW kept on building new-model prototypes (no fewer than 36 discarded types were shown to the Press in January 1968), but never stepped out of line.

When Nordhoff died, suddenly, in 1968, he was succeeded by Kurt Lotz, who found that the design cupboard was quite bare — except that there was now active co-operation with the Auto-Union combine in Bavaria, which VW had taken over from Mercedes-Benz in 1964.

Lotz moved rapidly to commission new small car designs, in which Porsche were involved. One, coded EA276 ('EA', incidentally, when translated from the German, means 'Development Order'), had a front-mounted Beetle flat-four engine and front-wheel drive. EA266 was a more advanced idea and had a four-cylinder engine, mounted on its side, under the rear seats. Throughout the project costs escalated, problems (of noise, service accessibility and smells) persisted, and when Rudolph Leiding took over from Kurt Lotz in October 1971, it was still in trouble.

Within weeks, Leiding cancelled EA266, and VW were back at the startline again, with the Beetle ageing rapidly, and a replacement urgently needed. Meantime, another small-medium project had already been schemed out, though not yet translated into metal — EA337. This was much more of a 'conventional' modern car, with a transverse front engine and front-wheel drive, and the style had already been completed by Giorgetto Giugiaro of ItalDesign.

It was under Leiding, therefore, that a 'crash' programme was initiated for a Beetle replacement. Porsche had been involved in the project stage, but VW at Wolfsburg did most of the design and development. The larger of the engines, however, actually came from Auto-Union of Ingolstadt, in Bavaria.

When VW took over Auto-Union, that company's boss was Rudolph Leiding, and the technical chief was Ludwig Kraus. The first car to carry the revived 'Audi' name (which had been dropped in 1939) was the 70, which used an engine originally designed at Mercedes-Benz by Kraus' team, for he had only recently moved to Ingolstadt.

Kraus and his team then designed a new medium-sized Audi (which became the 80, launched in 1972), for which a completely new four-cylinder engine, the Type 827 family, was produced. This was originally made in 1,296cc and 1,471cc sizes, in each case having a belt-driven single-overhead-camshaft layout, a cast-iron block, and a light-alloy cylinder head. Does this begin to sound familiar to GTI enthusiasts?

The Audi 80, of course, had its engine in line, and the gearbox behind it, but still drove the front wheels. It was an altogether larger car than EA337, but was also given a different, Giugiaro-styled, body shape and named the VW Passat, which was announced in 1973.

In the meantime, the new small-medium VW range was taking shape. Giugiaro came up with two distinctive styles on the same 7ft 10.5in wheelbase — a hatchback saloon with three or five doors, and a three-door hatchback coupe. The one car became the Golf in June 1974, the other the Scirocco, a few months earlier. The Golf was to be built at VW's headquarters at Wolfsburg, while the Scirocco would be totally assembled by the coachbuilders Karmann,

Starting point for the GTI engine was the 100bhp carburettor unit of the Audi 80GT introduced in 1974. Audi engine is north-south rather than transversely-mounted, as in the Golf. Later fuel injected engine from the GTI found its way back into the Audi as the 80GTE.

First appearance of the 'Sport Golf' as the GTI was in August 1975, just before the Frankfurt Motor Show. This car, above, was really a prototype and it took several months longer to produce the definitive production version. By then, prototype GTI badge had given way to the distinctive production style (right). Note plain steel wheels on these examples.

of Osnabruck.

Although the new car's wheelbase was the same as that of the Beetle, it was a completely and utterly different project in every other way. Here, in fact, was the first pure-bred VW combining a transversely-mounted water-cooled engine, front-mounted with front-wheel drive, and a modern, crisply detailed saloon body style. In fact, two engine families would be employed — the 1,093cc unit also being destined for a forthcoming generation of Audi-VWs (Audi 50 and VW Polo), while the 1,471cc engine was a modified version of the Audi 80 unit.

Allied to the 80's engine was a four-speed, all-synchromesh, all-indirect transmission, mounted end-on to the engine, to its left. Initially this engine was rated at 70bhp, but clearly there was a lot of potential (and some capacity stretch) still locked inside. Even in that state of tune, incidentally, the Golf 1500 was no slouch, for *Autocar's* road-testers achieved a 98mph maximum speed, and 0-60mph acceleration in 12.5 seconds.

Looking back, with the benefit of hindsight, we can see that the Golf's 'chassis' was ideal for its job, and an excellent basis for more powerful derivatives. The suspension, featuring MacPherson front struts and that characteristic 'torsion beam' rear end, was sturdy, the rack-and-pinion steering precise, and the mixed disc/drum braking system efficient.

Yet no more powerful version was planned. The engineers' 'Sport Golf' was exciting the fast-driving members of the development team, but hardly anyone else in the organization. There was, you see, no identifiable market sector for such a car to join. Only when early reports on the Golf had suggested that its perky performance and crisp handling had a sporting appeal did the marketing people sit up and take notice.

The 'Sport Golf' became an official Volkswagen project in May 1975, a year after the Golf had started full-scale production. The sales force was still not really enthusiastic. They reluctantly agreed to back the car on the understanding that only 5,000 would be built. That way, it would qualify as a Group 1 Production Touring Car for motor sport and they could spread the cars thinly among dealers throughout Europe. Within months of the GTI's launch they had to eat their words — eventually 5,000 were being built every *month*!

It was not, however, the best of times to sell the idea of a sporting car, either to management or to the public. The aftermath of the energy crisis was still making times hard for Europe's car makers (Volkswagen's production had been 2.1 million in 1971 and was slumping to 1.6 million in 1975). Nor was there any similar car's successful track record to point to, for support and encouragement.

When VW did decide to go ahead with limited production the 'Sport Golf' was about 80% ready. Herbert Schuster had just arrived at Volkswagen from Audi, and recalls that not long after approval it received its official name 'GTI'.

No-one can remember exactly from whence it came, but 'GT' was widely used and the suffix 'I' also had sporting connotations, even if it was not an abbreviation of the German for 'Injection'.

The first car to run actually had a Solex dual-choke carburettor and 100bhp engine tune — the power unit from the Audi 80GT. But 100bhp didn't really seem to be enough, so work began on a sporting version of the Type 827 that had already been adapted to Bosch K-Jetronic fuel injection to meet the

Right-hand drive evolution. Before 1979, Golf GTIs for the UK market were left-hand drive only and supplied to special order. T-registration (top left) was the first of the British editions and remained outwardly similar for two years (V and W reg.) 1981 car had five-speed gearbox, new alloy wheels came in 1982, and 1,800cc engine in 1983 (Y). 1984 special edition (A reg, bottom right) featured twin headlamp grille, metal sunroof and Pirelli sports wheels.

Mark 2 GTI, introduced in 1984, has new body shape plus factory-installed four headlamp system and twin exhausts. 6J × 14 wheels are perforated steel on standard version, in Germany, and (for three-door) in UK. Badge style, red bumper and grille line motif from Mark 1 remain.

stringent California exhaust emissions regulations. That boosted power to 110bhp — and, apart from the Golf, it also found a place in the car where it had started as the Audi 80GTE.

The final stages of the development took only a matter of months. There was some debate about the level of trim and equipment that such a car should have. Initial thoughts were that a GTI would be a car for the young, who would want performance rather than plush and would put value-for-money ahead of equipment and accessories. But the reaction to the idea from older and more affluent drivers changed their minds. The car would have to be distinctive — and well furnished.

The Volkswagen engineers still recall with pride that nothing that they had added to the GTI had to be abandoned before the model went on sale. Turbocharging was not seriously considered as no other manufacturer had yet adopted it in a small car and the technology was not fully understood. At the time, turbocharging was equated with poor low-speed torque and dreadful fuel consumption.

(Turbocharged Golfs, incidentally, have since been built, with power outputs up to 160bhp, but the company likes the smooth power delivery of the 16-valve engine much more. 'If we were ever to use forced induction,' one VW engineer told us, 'it would be with mechanical supercharging, not turbocharging....')

Not a lot of work was needed to trim the Golf's aerodynamic balance — a bigger front spoiler was added, but no tailgate reshaping was needed. 'The Scirocco *did* need a tail spoiler, and we could have added one to the Golf GTI if necessary, but it wasn't necessary', says Schuster. Rear disc brakes, too, were considered, but rejected, for with ventilated front discs VW reckoned that the original GTI had ample stopping power, even for high-speed German autobahns.

Once it had been approved, there was something of a rush to get the car on sale. The GTI shown at the Frankfurt Show in September 1975 was only a prototype, and production cars did not, in fact, become available until June 1976. The engineers themselves set the standards of performance and road behaviour. Herbert Schuster says that it was his team's responsibility, and that the car also had to meet every one of VW's normal standards.

Only six true prototypes had been built before the GTI project 'went official', then another 15 'durability' test cars were produced in the last few months. Among the many demanding tests which had to be carried out was a 100,000-kilometre (62,000-mile) run on one car, of which half this distance had to be at very high speeds, all on German autobahns. Not only that, but cars were sent for cold-weather testing to Scandinavia, and to Northern Africa for hot and dusty conditions. Nothing was left to chance.

Along the way the GTI development team expanded mightily. When the car was still a 'private enterprise' project, only four or five people were involved —

Five-door version of the Mark 1 GTI was available in some markets but not UK. VAG (United Kingdom) decided to import five-door version of the more spacious Mark 2, starting from 1985. This model is supplied standard with the Pirelli-style alloy wheels that are an option for the three-door GTI.

Opening up another new market — Volkswagen started the return to saloon-based convertibles with the open-topped version of the Golf, introduced in 1979. Made for VW by Karmann (they also produce the Scirocco body) it was available at first with a 1.6-litre GTI engine and luxury trim as the GLi.

later, as the grind of meeting every standard test took over, well over 100 specialists were involved.

By the time the GTI was ready for sale in 1976 it was, in truth, an 'engineer's car', and it showed. Almost everyone agreed that it was amazingly satisfying to drive — not only fast, but docile; not only comfortable and predictable, but with remarkable handling and response; not only a real trendsetter, but understated, even discreet, into the bargain. To everyone's eternal credit, it was neither overburdened with garish striping, badging, or other decoration, nor was its specification trimmed to get down to an arbitrary cost target.

In other words, everything in the GTI project had a purpose — the injection engine because it gave all the right results; the firmer, lowered, suspension because it gave the best roadholding; the wheelarch extensions because they covered the fatter wheels, rather than because they merely looked right. If only some other firms would learn from this process.....

It is interesting to hear from VW people that they don't believe that the 'GTI' process can be applied successfully to other cars in the range. The Golf GTI, they think, has a unique blend of size, type, feel and performance — a special

Though the Mark 2 Golf had arrived by 1984, the Convertible continued to be based on the Mark 1 — and will be, VW say, until at least 1987. This one, an 'all-black' special posed for a springtime publicity shot, is designated GTI and is mechanically like the hatchback, though not identical in behaviour.

character that 'just developed' as the car was refined.

There has, of course, been a Scirocco GTI — introduced at the same time as the Golf — and this shares the Golf floorpan, though in exchange for more traditionally sporting looks it provides much less accommodation for a higher price.

The nomenclature is also applied to the most powerful version of the Golf Convertible. This successor to the Beetle Cabriolet is produced by Karmann for VW, was introduced in 1979, and remained based on the 'Mark 1' Golf after the 'Mark 2' was launched in 1983. The engineers behind the GTI are slightly dismissive of the open-topped model, for although one version shares the

Powering past the opposition. Volkswagen's answer to their challengers in the expanding hot hatch market was to adopt a 16-valve twin-cam cylinder head for the 1.8-litre engine. Power was boosted to 139bhp and claimed performance up to 130mph. Identification markers are small '16V' badges, and deeper front spoiler, adopted for 1986 mainstream GTI.

110bhp fuel-injected engine, it is some 12% heavier than the saloon so that performance suffers. Furthermore, most of the extra weight is at the rear rather than over the driven wheels at the front, which means that suspension settings must be different. Inevitably, and despite the re-engineering undertaken by Karmann, the convertible bodyshell is not as rigid as the hatchback's, so the result is a car that does not have the 'pure' characteristics of a normal GTI. That is not to decry a car that was something of a trendsetter in its own right — small cabriolets followed from Ford, Talbot and others — and has a definite character of its own. But not everything that applies to the GTI, and not all the views expressed in this book, necessarily apply to the Golf Convertible.

Then there is the question of America, where Volkswagen have been making

Golfs since 1978. Not quite the same Golfs as in Europe, however, and until the advent of the Mark 2 body, not called Golfs but Rabbits. The US operation had its share of misfortune as well as misjudgment. The diesel-engined model, so enthusiastically received in the wake of the energy crisis, was a passing fashion. Somehow Volkswagen failed to hit the market right. The perceived qualities of German cars were lost when they became home-grown products with Detroit-style interiors. The GTI was introduced to America in 1982 as a way of boosting flagging sales. By 1984 it amounted to 40% of all Rabbit sales. *Road & Track* called it 'the best thing that has happened to Volkswagen since Americans succumbed to the Beetle'.

The lessons were learned. When the European Golf had a new shape, the American models adopted the family name — except the GTI which was simply a 'Volkswagen GTI'. In reality, though, it is a Golf, close in most respects to its European counterpart, though distinguished by rectangular headlamps and some cosmetic changes and with only 100bhp in deference to the USA's emissions-control regulations. It is also some 100lb heavier than the German-made car, which means that performance is rather less impressive (0-60mph acceleration in around 10 seconds, 1.5 seconds slower than the European GTI).

Americans are quite used to their cars going slower than the same models on the other side of the Atlantic. In its class in the US market the GTI still holds its own. Why, *Motor Trend* even nominated it their Car of the Year, 1985 — a contest between *domestic* cars in which it scored top marks in six out of nine categories of testing. They concluded: 'Other cars may rival it in one area or another, but nobody does it all in this class the way Volkswagen does.... an absolutely predictable, stable, sporting companion — a tiger in a three-piece suit.'

That is as good a definition as any of the spirit of the 'hot hatch'. And this is where it started....

Scirocco moved into its 'Mark 2' guise well before Golf and GTI version remained, sharing Golf GTI's 1.8-litre engine and the later alloy wheel design.

American version of the Mark 2 was designated simply Volkswagen GTI and so highly thought-of that the major magazine Motor Trend nominated it Car of the Year 1985. Close in style to its European counterpart, it features rectangular headlamps and different bumpers and alloy wheels.

At a glance, easy to confuse with the GTI — Golf Driver was a special edition Mark 1 Golf 1300 with the sports seats, steering wheel, instruments, wide wheels and tyres and black wing extensions of the GTI.

GTI — the numbers

In the first nine years of production, up to the end of 1984, 532,733 Golf and Rabbit GTIs were produced at Wolfsburg in Germany and Westmoreland, USA. Total UK registrations to the end of 1984 numbered 20,747. Germany, France and Switzerland are all bigger markets for the Golf GTI than Great Britain.

Production			UK registrations	
	Europe	**USA**		
1976	10,366			
1977	31,746			
1978	42,293		1978	22
1979	58,252		1979	1,573
1980	68,599		1980	1,449
1981	72,394		1981	3,834
1982	62,589	8,074	1982	3,830
1983	71,002	36,375	1983	6,148
1984	53,585	17,458	1984	3,885

The shape of Golfs to come? Volkswagen's Auto 2000 design study was shown at the 1981 Frankfurt Motor Show and demonstrated a shape for the hatchback of the future. It is said to have encouraged a late re-think of Vauxhall/Opel's new Astra/Kadett but VW's Mark 2 Golf proved much less radical. Perhaps Mark 3 will be closer to this turn-of-the-century idea.

Technical examination

What made the Golf a suitable case for GTI treatment — an appraisal by Jeffrey Daniels

JEFFREY DANIELS is a highly-respected technical writer of wide experience and interest, ranging from aeronautical to automotive engineering. He developed car testing techniques at *Motoring Which,* became technical editor of *Autocar,* and has worked in management at the UK headquarters of Citroen and Datsun. Now freelance, he is engineering editor of the monthly enthusiast magazine *Performance Car.*

The GTI is successful as a sporting car because of the soundness of the basic Golf chassis. This mirrored cutaway drawing is the Mark 2 with carburettor engine; fuel injection apart, the main difference for the GTI is the use of disc brakes all round.

Once Volkswagen had taken the decision to go front-wheel drive, the design team laid down a chassis of such quality that the development of versions with more power — of the GTI, in fact — was almost inevitable. It is therefore worth looking at the basic Golf first of all, before progressing to the changes that were made in order to turn a quick, compact family car into the forerunner of a whole new breed of sports saloons.

There were three notable things about the Golf from an engineering point of view. First, it had a body outstanding for its combination of stiffness and low weight. Second, its engine was not only modern and efficient, but capable of being 'stretched'. Third, its suspension was deceptive in its seeming simplicity, but was actually subtle and effective, especially at the rear.

Where the body was concerned, the Golf was one of the first cars to take full advantage of computer stressing techniques, which in turn encouraged its designers to exploit the weight-saving potential of front-wheel drive. Whatever the arguments which then raged concerning the merits of the layout on the grounds of stability, handling, steering weight and so on, precious few observers bothered to point out that in a body where all the drive and front suspension stresses (and by far the larger proportion of the braking stress too) could be contained within a small but strong box based on the front bulkhead, inner wing skins and engine mounting longerons, the rest of it did little more than trail behind. Thus the cabin could be made very light indeed, within the constraints imposed by the need for both rigidity under impact, and for accuracy of rear suspension location.

Wolfsburg's designers certainly appreciated that, and the result was that when the Golf emerged its most basic version weighed comfortably less than 1,700lb. Despite the weight which was inevitably added in the creation of the GTI, the first of its kind to be tested by *Autocar* still scaled only 1,862lb at the kerb: usefully less than the then-current Escort RS2000, for example.

The larger of the two Golf engines was not entirely new, since it had been used in more conservative in-line front-drive form in the Audi 80 since that car's announcement in 1972. All that had been done in carrying it over to the Golf was to adapt it, where necessary, to the needs of transverse rather than in-line installation.

While modern in design, the engine was hardly revolutionary in concept. The alloy head carried a toothed belt-driven overhead camshaft acting directly on in-line valves through bucket tappets. Unlike the smaller (and brand-new for the Golf) 1.1-litre engine, the 1.5-litre was not crossflow. That meant that in some degree, efficiency was being sacrificed for ease of installation and maintenance. The engine broke with Beetle tradition in having mildly over-square dimensions with a bore of exactly 80mm and a stroke of 76.5mm, giving an actual capacity of 1,471cc. Power output was 70bhp at 5,800rpm. The drive was taken through a four-speed, all-indirect gearbox in line with the crankshaft, and out through a spur gear to the final drive aft of, and partly beneath, the rear-canted engine.

If anything, the Golf suspension provoked more criticism than praise, which showed how little people understood it. At the front, the Volkswagen engineers adopted MacPherson struts with all the refinements which other people (like Ford) had learned through years of sometimes painful experience. A

Contrast underbonnet of Mark 1 GTI, above, with the cutaway drawing of the Mark 2's engine. In basis they are the same but the plumbing for the fuel injection system has been relocated with the inlet plenum on the left rather than the right. With inlet and exhaust manifolds on the same side, rather than in the theoretically more efficient crossflow configuration, transverse installation is made more convenient.

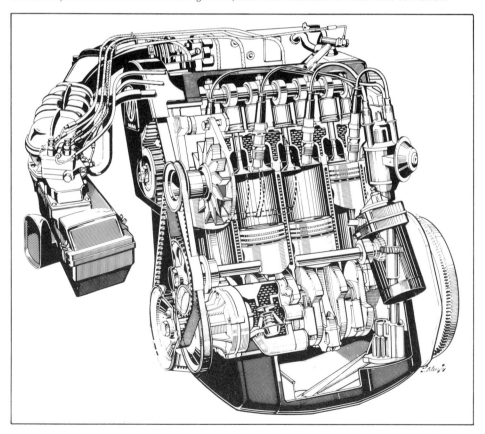

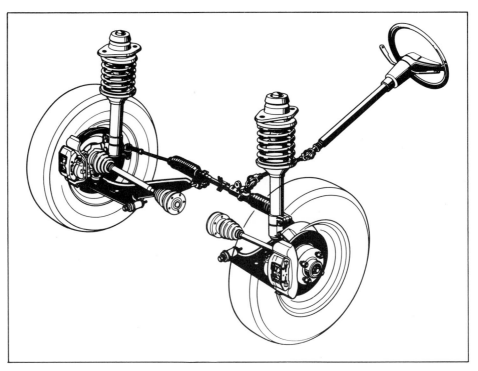

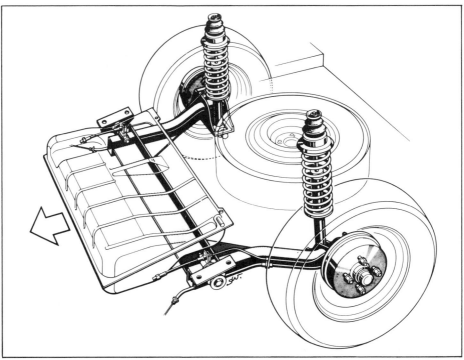

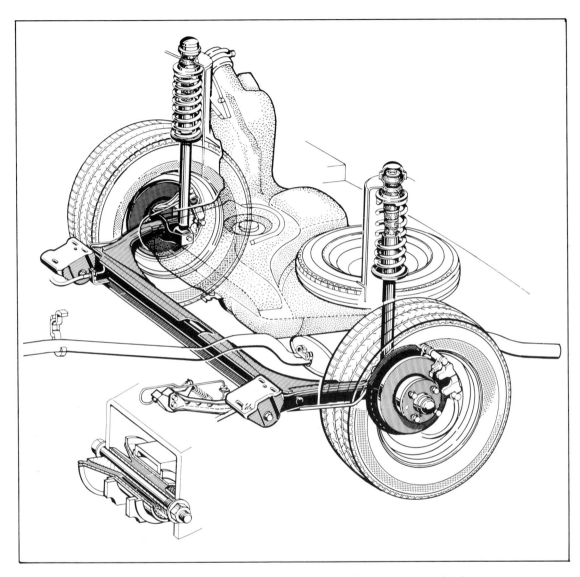

Front and rear suspension layouts illustrated left are basic Mark 1 Golf; GTI differs in having ventilated front disc brakes and anti-roll bar at the rear. Compare with Mark 2 GTI rear suspension above.Similar in configuration, the section of the 'torsion beam' is quite different; note elaborate bushing at its mountings. Moulded plastic fuel tank enabled Mark 2 to carry two more gallons in more-or-less the same location.

combination of modern bush materials and a coil spring axis offset from that of the damper, for instance, overcame the original MacPherson tendency to suffer from 'stiction', which caused a jerky low-speed ride. Volkswagen added a development of its own in the form of the negative-offset steering geometry — that is, with the steering axis meeting the ground outboard of the centre point of the tyre contact patch — which had been shown in the Audi 80 and VW Passat to confer a degree of self-correcting stability when braking with one side of the car on a slippery surface, or with one front tyre punctured.

It was the rear suspension which raised most eyebrows. It was not entirely new, since it had already been seen in the Scirocco, but it was only when the same components appeared in the Golf that their significance began to sink in. What the Volkswagen engineers had started with, beyond doubt, was the conventional front-drive thinking of the time which argued that unless, like Alfasud, Lancia and Saab, you used a light 'dead' axle at the rear, your best bet was to adopt a pair of simple trailing arms together with an anti-roll bar to provide some measure of rear roll stiffness and cut down the natural understeer of the front-drive configuration. It clearly occurred to somebody at Wolfsburg that by locating the anti-roll bar more solidly to the trailing arms it could be made to do a second and very important job. It would take out many of the stresses acting transversely on each arm, plus those trying to twist them out of line, leaving the suspension bushes merely to locate the whole U-shaped assembly fore-and-aft and sideways. At the same time the rear roll stiffness could be accurately tuned through careful design of the crossbeam which, in the Golf, took the form of a T-section lying on its side with its stalk towards the front. This enabled the beam to be made very strong in bending (thus keeping the trailing arms parallel) without making it too stiff in torsion.

As a piece of design, this rear suspension had much to recommend it. It was light and cheap, but better still it played off stresses one against the other within the U-frame and allowed the body to be made that much lighter. These virtues may not have been immediately evident to people who accused Volkswagen of 'throwing away the advantages of independent rear suspension', but they were quickly appreciated by rival design teams, whose interpretations of the theme began to appear three or four years later.

These, then, were the design cornerstones of the car which was to grow into the Golf GTI. The Golf was launched in the middle of 1974; the GTI appeared in September 1975, which showed that its engineering had been well under way even before the basic car appeared. As we have seen in the first chapter, the original Frankfurt Show car was actually an official prototype and it took another nine months to get the GTI into production. Even so, it was a very fast development programme, made possible because of the use of major parts already engineered.

Early in 1974 there appeared a developed version of the Audi 80, the 80GT, which among other improvements featured a stretched version of the original 1.5-litre engine: once again the Audi was being used as a technical stalking-horse for the Golf. All that had been done was to lengthen the stroke by 3mm to 79.5 mm, making the unit almost exactly 'square' and giving it a capacity of 1,588cc. In the 80GT the engine was still equipped with a twin-choke Solex carburettor but, clearly, a good deal had been done to improve the unit's

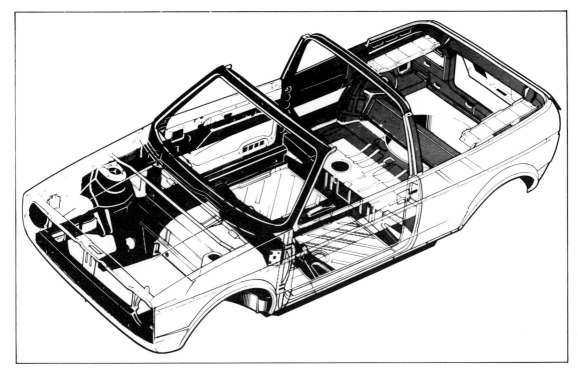

Golf Convertible needed considerable revisions to the bodyshell to maintain adequate strength and stiffness with open top. Roll-over protection, seat belt mounting and hood location all demanded the central hoop. Convertible's boot is restricted and access is through a small hatch.

breathing since it produced exactly 100bhp at 6,000rpm. That engine would happily have gone into the Golf to produce a quick car in its own right, but in fact the 80GT was no more than a development stepping-stone. The next stage was to add Bosch K-Jetronic fuel injection and produce the first definitive, 110bhp GTI unit.

The GTI retained the 1,588cc capacity of the 80GT engine plus the measures which had been taken to improve the breathing: larger-diameter valves and Heron combustion chambers recessed in the piston crowns, rather than the original bathtub shape. The inlet and exhaust manifolds were new, giving improved gas flow while also leaving enough room for the injection pump, driven by an extra pulley inserted in the run of the camshaft-drive toothed belt. Such was the resulting smoothness and eagerness to rev that Volkswagen deemed it essential to fit an ignition cut-out operating at 7,000rpm. Audi experience had also suggested the need for improved oil flow and for the provision of an oil-cooling radiator. The GTI produced 57% more power than was available in the 1.5-litre Golf GLS, and a worthwhile improvement in torque as well. At the time of its announcement, and for some time afterwards, the drive continued to be taken through a four-speed gearbox.

The resemblance of the new Golf to the old was
intentionally close but belies the amount of work
that went into the re-style. Concept sketches,
right, show some ideas that were not pursued,
like a soft plastic nose section. Full-size clay
models gave three-dimensional form to the new
shape and the more spacious interior. Cost of
developing the Mark 2 was put at £250 million.

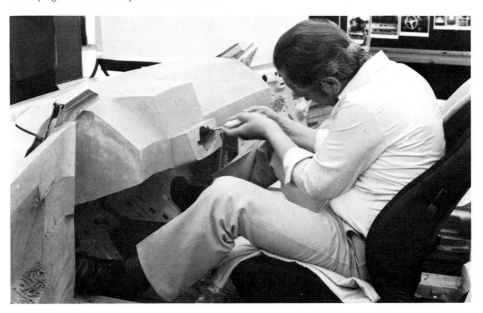

The basic Golf chassis needed tuning, hardly more, to accept the extra power. The first requirement was more rubber on the road, which was duly supplied in the form of 175-section tyres to replace the standard 155s, worn on wider 5½-inch rims. Spring rates were increased, the standard dampers changed for specially rated Bilsteins and the roll stiffness further increased, at the front by fitting a larger-diameter anti-roll bar and at the rear by adding a small supplementary bar nested into the original torsion crossbeam. At first the ride height was left as standard, Volkswagen engineers feeling that the car already had a sufficiently low centre of gravity for good handling — and, undoubtedly, that any reduction in wheel travel would have noticeable consequences for the ride — but before long popular demand caused it to be reduced by 20mm, which also helped to give the car a more distinctive look. There was one further improvement in the form of a much deeper (though still discreet by some standards!) 'chin' spoiler, which was claimed to reduce front-end lift by 65lb at 100mph, ensuring positive high-speed stability.

The standard Golf braking system was also uprated, plain front discs giving way to ventilated units together with a bigger vacuum servo. The small rear drums, however, were left as they were: overall this was a mistake, since the brakes were almost the only aspect of the first-series GTI to be consistently criticized in road tests.

Be that as it may, the Golf GTI quickly became something of a 'cult' car in those few markets where it was sold. It became quite a sore point in Britain especially that the car was not made in right-hand-drive form, an omission that was not corrected until mid-1979, almost four years after the original launch.

Such was the rightness of the concept that very little had changed in the interim, other than the inevitable adoption of low-profile 175/70-13in tyres. One very important change was on the way, however, forced by the advent of the second great energy crisis of 1978-79 (and also, some would suggest, by high-speed cruising noise levels); a five-speed gearbox was finally made available. The party line at the time was that the fifth gear permitted economical cruising while leaving the four lower ratios intact for sporting GTI-type driving. The five-speed transmission became standard for the 1980 model year, together with attractive alloy wheels.

The market created by the Golf GTI was too lucrative not to have spawned rival models, and by the early 1980s Volkswagen was looking to ways of keeping the Golf a step ahead of the pack. The obvious move was to add power, which in turn required more engine capacity if specific power was not to be increased at the expense of reliability. This was the approach they broadly followed although, once again, VW engineers indulged in a measure of lateral thinking. The GTI engine was extensively reworked to increase capacity: the bore was opened out slightly to 81mm, while the stroke went all the way to 86.4mm to give a swept volume of 1,781cc. The longer stroke meant a new

Styling sketches from the Wolfsburg design department show ideas for front and back of Mark 2: two and four round headlamps and a rectangular lamp front not unlike final US version. High-set tail lamp configuration was adopted. VW considered 10 design proposals for the Mark 2, including one from Giugiaro's ItalDesign that produced the original Golf shape; an in-house study won.

crankshaft, and the opportunity was taken to improve its balancing and to fit a torsional vibration damper. Stresses were reduced by a careful lightening of many components including the pistons and connecting rods, while the longer rods themselves helped reduce out-of-balance accelerations. Advantage was taken of the greater bore size to increase valve diameter slightly yet again, while the combustion chamber shape was subtly changed — in the light of extensive Volkswagen research into lean-burn technology — to allow the compression

Volkswagen announced their 16-valve engine in the Scirocco back in 1983 but it didn't go into production (in Golf and Scirocco GTIs) until 1985. There were extensive design revisions in the interim.

ratio to be increased to 10:1.

The surprise was that all this work resulted in just 2bhp more! What Volkswagen had decided to do, very wisely, was to boost torque rather than power in the interests of flexibility and mid-range acceleration rather than maximum speed. Thus the valve timing overlap was to some extent unwound; the new engine's 112bhp was delivered at 5,800rpm instead of 6,100 while its 109lb/ft of torque at 3,500rpm contrasted with the former 101lb/ft at no less than 5,000rpm, and even this does no more than suggest the new-found flatness of the torque curve. Allied to a higher final drive, it endowed the GTI with better economy and quieter running, while the higher torque gave notably better acceleration through the gears. Maximum speed, on the other hand, was very little higher — as you would expect.

The next technical move was significant: the replacement of the original Golf by the Mark 2. The visual similarity of the new Golf body to its predecessor disguised the fact that its drag coefficient had dropped from 0.40 to 0.34, something which was bound to be reflected in maximum speed. At the same time weight had increased, not surprisingly since the new car was 3in longer in its wheelbase, 6.7in longer and 2.2in wider overall. Thus acceleration had to suffer slightly. However, further work on the engine had fattened up the torque curve even more. While peak power remained at 112bhp (now at only 5,500rpm) the new peak torque figure was 114lb/ft at 3,100rpm.

As the first road test results for the new-shape GTI appeared, it was clear that in practice the acceleration had suffered hardly at all: 60mph was still reached well inside 9 seconds. Maximum speed was significantly up, but maybe the most striking thing of all was the general agreement that even with the kind of treatment meted out by professional road-testers, the new GTI still returned better than 30mpg.

There was equal agreement that the new braking system — discs all round at last — was far superior. The GTI was certainly well capable of exploiting the grip of the bigger 185/60-14in tyres. It is a tribute to the soundness of the original suspension design that it was changed only in detail, to increase wheel travel in search of improved ride comfort and to filter out more of the road noise. The

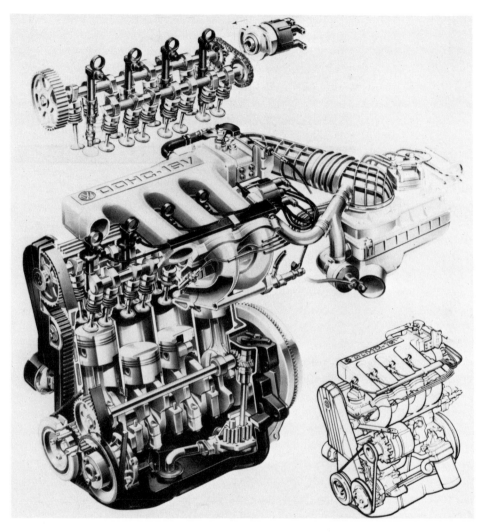

Elements of the twin overhead camshaft four-valves-per-cylinder engine of the GTI 16V. One camshaft is belt-driven in the conventional way, the other by chain at the opposite end of the cylinder head. Vertical exhaust valves are paired with inlet valves inclined at 25deg. from the vertical — efficient and compact.

section of the torsion crossbeam was changed to an open channel and the design of the rear attachment points and bushes was altered to allow a degree of rear suspension 'self-correction' — the slight change in rear wheel attitude tending to cancel out the car's natural roll-oversteer effect. Finally, since the car was heavier than before and deployed even more torque, the option of power-assistance of the rack-and-pinion steering became desirable — and was introduced in the 1986 model year.

The final chapter of the GTI story — to date — was the long-awaited arrival of the 16-valve engine. A 16-valve Scirocco had been announced in 1983, but proved elusive when it came to actual production: it transpired that Volkswagen engineers had opted for another year of development, mainly in order to be able to offer both 'normal' and catalyst-equipped versions in markets increasingly overshadowed by severe exhaust emissions standards.

From a more basic engineering viewpoint the 16-valve engine was interesting because it represented a novel way of converting a standard eight-valve engine to four-valves-per-cylinder configuration. Twin overhead camshafts become a virtual necessity (if one excepts the 1970s Triumph Dolomite Sprint with its multitude of rockers). The usual technique is to extend the chain or toothed-belt run to drive two camshaft sprockets instead of one, but Volkswagen sought to save space in its tight transverse engine installation by retaining a toothed-belt drive to a single camshaft, and 'slaving' the second shaft to the first by a drive at the other end of the engine. The original system used a gear drive between the two camshafts, but in its definitive form the 16-valve emerged with a short chain linking two tiny sprockets: a quieter solution and one even less demanding of space.

The 16-valve head was entirely new, of course, and of interest also because its valve layout was not symmetrical. Instead, its inlet valves leaned 25 degrees away from the cylinder centreline, while the exhaust valves were upright (but offset). As a result, the combustion chamber had a gentle wedge-shape, something which again reflects Volkswagen's long-standing interest in basic combustion research. The 16-valve also marked a significant move to hydraulic tappets for the sake of consistent valve clearance.

Beneath the new head, the familiar 1,781cc engine was largely retained, which emphasizes the gains to be had from going to four-valves-per-cylinder: not only was peak power up from 112 to 139bhp (129 with a catalyst exhaust system) but there was also an 8% increase in peak torque. Standard GTI gearing was retained, except for a slightly lower top gear, but with the engine speed governor set at 7,200rpm the extra performance potential of the 16-valve is clear enough; sufficient at the very least to have made Volkswagen carry out another extensive round of suspension lowering (by 10mm) and tuning.

For the present, the 16-valve is the peak of Golf GTI technology. However, Volkswagen has a habit of taking a further decisive step each time the opposition looks like catching up, and there is no shortage of future options available — the most obvious being four-wheel drive, where the VAG Group retains more expertise than any other concern. Anti-lock braking and supercharging are two other areas which may be explored. The only certain thing is that the Golf GTI will defend its position by taking its engineering even further along the road to high performance matched by efficiency.

Specifications

Mark 1

Engine Four-cylinder, in-line; cast iron block, aluminium alloy cylinder head. Five main bearings. Single overhead camshaft driven by toothed belt. Bosch K-Jetronic fuel injection.

— 1976-1982
1,588cc, bore 79.5mm, stroke 80.0mm. Compression ratio 9.5:1 110bhp (DIN) at 6,100rpm. 101lb/ft torque at 5,000rpm.

— 1982-1984
1,781cc, bore 81.0mm, stroke, 86.4mm. Compression ratio 10:1. 112bhp (DIN) at 5,800rpm. 109lb/ft torque at 3,500rpm.

Transmission

— 1976-1981
Four-speed, all indirect, with synchromesh.
Ratios (mph per 1,000rpm): 1st 3.45 (5.0); 2nd 1.94 (8.9); 3rd 1.37 (12.6); 4th 0.97 (17.3). Final drive ratio 3.7.

— 1981-1983
Five-speed, all indirect, with synchromesh
Ratios (mph per 1,000rpm): 1st 3.45 (4.9); 2nd 2.12 (8.0); 3rd 1.44 (11.7); 4th 1.13 (14.9); 5th 0.91 (18.5). Final drive ratio 3.9.

— 1982-1984 (1800 engine)
Five-speed, all indirect, with synchromesh
Ratios (mph per 1,000 rpm): 1st 3.45 (5.25);2nd 2.12 (8.5); 3rd 1.44 (12.6), 4th (16.0); 5th 0.91 (19.85). Final drive ratio 3.65.

Suspension
Front: Independent, with MacPherson struts and lower wishbones, coil springs and anti-roll bar.
Rear: Semi-independent, with trailing arms and torsion beam, coil springs, telescopic shock absorbers and anti-roll bar.

Steering
Rack and pinion, 3.3 turns from lock to lock.

Brakes
Front: 9.4in dia. ventilated discs. Rear: 7.1in dia. drums. Vacuum servo (crossbar transfer to right-hand drive).

Wheels
5½J 13in diameter, with 175/70 HR radial ply tyres (1983 'campaign' model 6J 14 in dia. with 185/60HR tyres). Tyre pressures (175/70) 24psi front and rear.

Capacities
Fuel tank 9.9gal (45 litres).
Cooling system 11.4 pints.
Engine sump 6 pints 10W/40 oil.
Gearbox and final drive 2.2 pints SAE80.

Dimensions
Overall length: 146.5in. Overall width: 63.5in.
Overall height: 55.5in. Wheelbase: 94.5in.
Front track: 54.7in. Rear track: 53.0in.
Max payload 930lb. Kerb weight 1,862lb.

Mark 2

Engine Four-cylinder, in-line; cast iron block, aluminium alloy cylinder head. Five main bearings. Single overhead camshaft driven by toothed belt. Bosch K-Jetronic fuel injection. 1,781cc, bore 81.0mm, stroke 86.4mm Compression ratio 10:1. 112bhp (DIN) at 5,500 rpm. 114lb/ft torque at 3,100rpm.

Transmission
Five-speed, all indirect, with synchromesh.
Ratios (mph per 1,000rpm): 1st 3.45 (5.5); 2nd 2.12 (8.9); 3rd 1.44 (13.1); 4th 1.13 (16.7); 5th 0.89 (21.3). Final drive ratio 3.67.

Suspension
Front: Independent, with MacPherson struts and lower wishbones, coil springs and anti-roll bar.
Rear: Semi-independent, with trailing arms and torsion beam, coil springs, telescopic dampers and anti-roll bar.

Steering
Rack and pinion, 3.75 turns from lock to lock.

Brakes
Front: 9.4in dia. ventilated discs. Rear: 8.9in dia. solid discs. Vacuum servo.

Wheels
6in wide, 14in diameter with 185/60HR radial ply tyres. Tyre pressures: 29psi front, 26psi rear (normal driving).

Capacities
Fuel tank 12.1gal (55 litres).
Cooling system 11.1 pints.
Engine sump 5.5 pints.

Dimensions
Overall length: 156.9in. Overall width: 66.1in.
Overall height: 55.3in. Wheelbase: 97.4in.
Front track: 56.0in. Rear track: 56.0in.
Max payload 1,124lb. Kerb weight: 2,063lb.

16V

Engine Four-cylinder in-line cast iron block, aluminium alloy cylinder head. Five main bearings. Twin overhead camshafts, one driven by toothed belt, other by chain across head. Four valves per cylinder. Bosch K-Jetronic fuel injection. 1,781cc, bore 81.0mm, stroke 86.4mm. Compression ratio 10:1 139bhp (DIN) at 6,100rpm. 133lb/ft torque at 4,600rpm.

Other specifications as Mark 2.

Assessment by Miles

John Miles gets to grips with the 'Mark 2' encompassing experience of earlier GTIs

W hen it first appeared, the GTI totally redefined the performance and handling of a sporting family car. Other manufacturers followed its lead — surprisingly slowly — but the Golf GTI remained the car to beat.

I have test-driven all the versions over the years, from the original left-hand-drive models, through the 1800 to the current Mark 2 and 16-valve. This is an assessment of the 1985 GTI with its regular engine, but with reference to my experiences with other models of the type. The Mark 2 may have lost the angular balance of line of the original version, but it offers much better rear-seat legroom and luggage space and its softer lines have achieved a remarkable improvement in aerodynamic performance.

When the engine capacity was increased from 1,588cc to 1,781cc most of the larger swept volume came from a longer stroke. The first thing critics looked for was a deterioration in the marvellous smoothness we had become so used to in the 1600. There was none. There was only a small increase in power, but a hefty improvement in torque and the whole torque curve was much fatter. The result is a superbly flexible engine, yet one that still sings happily up to the rev-limiter — and that's nothing compared with the new 16-valve GTI unit, which will scream to over 7,000rpm with the same easy willingness and lack of vibration.

I have never seen an eight-valve GTI do the claimed 119mph, more like 115mph for a good one, and 0-60mph in around 8.5sec is an average figure. Measured performance seems nothing out of the ordinary, but it is the way the GTI delivers the goods that is so appealing. Mile after mile you can thrash it and it feels absolutely unburstable. Gearing is ideally arranged to give maximum speed in fifth (rather than the overdrive top gear seen on some competitors) and complementing the engine's eager response is a set of fairly close intermediate ratios that leaves no gaps in the acceleration curve. In real terms it

JOHN MILES has the rare talent of combining world-class race driving skills with top-flight technical journalism. A member of the Lotus Grand Prix team in 1969 and 1970, and subsequently works driver for BRM, Chevron and others, he retired from racing and joined the *Autocar* test and technical team in 1977. He is now a freelance journalist and engineering consultant.

Flashback to the original GTI — then, as with the latest version, its behaviour on the test track was praised for its high performance and handling balance.

goes as well as anything but a 2-litre Fiat Strada Abarth 130TC or the more powerful turbocharged Lancia Delta HF and Ford Escort RS — but then turbo power can never have quite the same response as a good normally aspirated unit.

Driven hard, the GTI engine is not quiet, but emits an appealing rasp typical of well-matched intake and exhaust systems, but the trade-off for this does seem to be the slight exhaust resonance at around 4,000rpm, which mars motorway cruising refinement. Above that it hums along happily at any speed up to its maximum.

Cruising speeds of 80 to 100mph (where permitted!) seem natural for the GTI because of its stability, handling and ride; the old Golf was good in this respect, but the new one is better. It has more wheel travel, revised springing and damping, and a longer wheelbase, but perhaps most critical to the new Golf's competence is the redesigned rear axle system. The rubber axle-to-chassis mountings for the interconnected trailing arms are arranged to counter the deflection steer that can easily occur in a system where the wheel is effectively attached to an arm overhung from its mountings.

Just about all the pundits praise the GTI for its balance and traction, and for me a real chance to prove this came during some filming at Thruxton circuit where the BBC TV had lined one up against three of the opposition: Vauxhall Astra GTE, Ford Escort XR3i and Fiat Strada 130TC. A testing circuit, and drizzle all day, added to the fun. The GTI could be thrown into the third-gear right/left Campbell and Cobb curves with a kind of easy predictability. It is in these extreme conditions that the GTI maintains gentle understeer unless the driver finds himself using a little too much road. Then, adjust the throttle and the car responds by gently 'tucking in', or moving to a little oversteer if the throttle is snapped shut. Its manners are always gentle and progressive; the driver can maintain a decent power setting rather than lift off to sort things out. Through the fast sweeping curves of Thruxton there is less understeer than in slow corners, but the essential elements of handling and stability remain. In and out of the chicane the GTI would turn in and put its power down better than all the others. The wet weather highlighted Fiat handling that was dominated by

VAG (United Kingdom)'s Press Department have taken to introducing new versions of the GTI to journalists at Prescott hill-climb. Here the 1800 Mark 1 makes its sure-footed way up the twisting course.

understeer, and the Ford's comparative lack of traction, while the Vauxhall did not have the same mid-corner stability in the fast sections. The real test came when we ran the cars four-up — adding a cameraman, a sound man and a continuity lady. Apart from having the most rear seat-room, the GTI remained the most stable and predictable of the bunch. Even the TV crew offered comment to that effect.....

Essentially what the GTI has is an unusual blend of stability *and* balance, whereas some others achieve their stability at the expense of balance. With 185/60-14 Pirelli P6 tyres as standard there is no more rubber on the road than with the opposition; it simply seems to use the available grip more effectively. Instead of understeer and wheelspin forming the limit, you can often haul the GTI back nearer to the inside of the turn even when the front tyres are sliding.

One quirk is its slightly 'loose' centre steering feel, and the fairly sharp build-up of effort either side of straight-ahead. On the road, this is something that seems to go hand in hand with an irritating oscillation of the steering when accelerating hard away from rest with the wheel slightly off-centre. With more lock, the steering loads normally build up nicely with cornering force. The GTI whistles surefootedly through a series of S-bends. Make a right at a T-junction

Behind the wheel of the Mark 2. Generally, Miles praises the control and facia layout and even the sequential 'trip computer' operated from the right-hand stalk and displaying on a liquid crystal screen below the warning light cluster.

on a wet road and it takes a deliberately rough throttle to generate any wheelspin; but when this happens with quite a lot of lock on there are occasions when the normal self-centering effect vanishes.

Another trait is the tendency to wander slightly with some lightening of the steering when accelerating hard in second or third gear — say, in fast overtaking. It is harmless enough but a rather eerie characteristic until you get used to it and certainly more prevalent when there are undulations, road cambers, or raised white lines to start it off.

You only have to look at the action shots to see that the GTI's roll control is nothing special and, if anything, the high-set driving position accentuates the lean perceived by the driver. The important thing is not the amount of roll so much as the rate of roll, and this is tolerably well controlled by damping and the use of rubber and polyurethane 'spring aids' (effectively very progressive bump stops).

Approximately $3\frac{3}{4}$ turns of the steering wheel cover an averagely tight turning circle, so there is not too much arm twirling for right-angle bends. It is far from light when manoeuvring, though.

I suspect that straight-line stability is aided by good aerodynamic balance,

Facia of later Mark 1 GTI shows obvious similarities to the Mark 2 opposite but has a less integrated layout. This 1982 1800 has the same kind of trip computer as the current cars.

That controversial 'spacesaver' spare wheel avoids a hump in the boot floor and although perfectly satisfactory when used according to the instructions (not more than 50mph), it is designed only for short-term emergency use. Some owners prefer the reassurance of a full-sized spare.

because the car shrugs off all but the worst cross-winds and bow waves that trucks produce.

Mark 2 GTI's require much lower braking efforts than the Mark 1, and with the new discs on the back, braking presents no problems with fade or balance. My experience is that GTIs vary a bit in ride quality. For most conditions there is an excellent blend of damping, control and comfort, so it is always rather a surprise to feel the fidgety movements that can occur over road joints and minor unevennesses in apparently smooth concrete surfaces. Road-generated noise is also something of a paradox, because although bump-thump on potholes is moderate, the level of tyre roar at motorway speeds is above the norm.

Refinement? I find the GTI an odd mixture. At first it seems very refined — town motoring and medium-speed touring — but at constant high speeds, road-induced noise and the rather 'thrummy' note (especially at 4,000rpm) from under the bonnet seem to combine. It is mild enough, but can creep up on the driver who is sensitive to these things.

Ergonomically, it remains one of the best, but for my taste the gear lever is rather too low — or the seat too high. It means reaching down slightly, and as a result one tends to push down and forward when selecting first — thus all too probably selecting reverse. Judged by the very best standards, the shift is also a little sticky and ponderous. The clutch is sweet in operation, but pedal efforts needed are among the highest in the class.

Few could fault VW stalk controls and, thankfully, VW have not succumbed to the stupidity of digital instruments. I have always liked their 'minimal' instrument pack (speedometer and rev-counter with inset fuel contents and water temperature) and the little panel of warning lights for battery charge, indicators, oil pressure and main beam. Moreover, you don't need a degree in electronics to operate the on-board 'computer' — you simply press the end of the right-hand stalk to get sequential read-outs of journey time, distance, oil and ambient temperatures, plus average speed and mpg (the latter not to be taken too seriously.....), and the liquid crystal display also provides a clock.

For night driving, the new GTI's four-lamp halogen system seems just that bit more piercing than most on full beam.

There are those who complain of poor rear-quarter visibility, but the thick 'C'

Road manners remain good even in the rain, but it is disappointing that the windscreen wipers remain set for left-hand drive on UK models. This picture shows a Mark 2 GTI on test at Prescott with Jeremy Walton — author of Chapter 7 — at the wheel. Jeremy is reigning VAG Prescott 'champion' with a time of 55.7sec in the 16V.

The GTI 16-valve powers round a hairpin, waving a rear wheel in the air. Less alarming for the driver than it looks from the outside, it emphasizes the speed with which this most powerful of GTIs can cover a winding road.

panels have not bothered me much, if only because the door mirrors give a decent field of vision. But why couldn't VW convert the wipers to right-hand drive?

Output, airflow and temperature control in VW's new air-blending heating and ventilation system are all excellent, yet it fails to provide a 'split' facility for those of us who sometimes like warm feet and cold noses. I will argue with VW's policy of fitting a lightweight spare wheel with all the speed and handling limitations that involves. I'd rather have a hump in the rear floor covering a normal spare, and the small sacrifice in luggage carrying capacity (of which the GTI has plenty).

No car is perfect, and it is only when you live with one for long periods that you learn by how much the good outweighs the bad. With the GTI you can be reasonably sure that body and mechanicals will be more reliable than most. It is hard to find a better-finished car in its class; I have not seen one where the paint is poor or the doors do not fit beautifully. There are a few weak points in its dynamic behaviour, but they are small compared with its strengths. I have never been in one where the engine does not catch immediately from hot or cold and drive away without fault. You have trouble making a GTI do worse than 30mpg, so with a 12-gallon tank it will do at least 300 miles between fuel stops.

The GTI cult built up because it was the first of its kind and quickly earned an enviable reputation for performance, handling and quality. It may be one of the most expensive cars in its class, but in so many important areas it still comes out on top.

Performance

The GTI has been widely praised in road tests published throughout Europe. In Britain, the definitive tests are those carried out by the weekly magazines *Autocar* and *Motor* and these figures are published with the kind permission of their respective Editors:

	Mark 1 1600 4-speed		Mark 1 1600 5-speed	Mark 1 1800	Mark 2	
	Autocar	Motor	Autocar	Autocar	Autocar	Motor
Max. speed	108	108	111	113	114	115
0-30mph	3.3	3.3	2.9	2.5	3.0	3.0
0-40mph	5.4	4.9	4.6	3.8	4.5	4.3
0-50mph	7.4	7.0	6.1	5.6	6.2	6.0
0-60mph	9.8	9.6	9.0	8.3	8.6	8.3
0-70mph	14.3	13.0	12.1	11.1	11.3	11.0
0-80mph	19.3	17.0	16.1	14.2	15.3	14.4
0-90mph	28.7	22.7	21.9	19.4	20.5	18.5
0-100mph	—	35.3	33.9	26.1	29.0	26.6
Standing $\frac{1}{4}$-mile	17.3	17.2	16.9	16.2	16.6	16.5
Standing kilometre	32.3	32.0	31.5	30.2	30.8	30.5
Overall mpg	27.3	28.5	27.2	28.5	29.0	30.6

NEED A NEW PART? NEED A GOOD PRICE? NEED IT DONE QUICKLY? YOU NEED TO COME TO US.

What a shame to spoil your Volkswagen with a replacement part that isn't up to the standard of the original.

Especially when the Genuine Volkswagen parts are readily available from your Volkswagen dealership. Where you'll get first-class service, and fitting by trained mechanics who know the vehicles like real specialists should.

Just ask for a quotation and you'll be given a written Price Guarantee. So when you come to have the job done you know there will be no hidden extras.

And if you need a small repair which takes 45 minutes or less, every effort will be made to give you immediate attention.

Next time you need a service, repair or parts, you need to come to us.

WHO ELSE CAN GIVE YOU A GUARANTEED PRICE AND THE GENUINE PART.

Audi Volkswagen, National After Sales,
V.A.G (United Kingdom) Limited, Yeomans Drive, Blakelands, Milton Keynes, MK14 5AN.

Additional enjoyment

A critical look at some of the accessories that can enhance your comfort and driving pleasure

As it comes from the factory, the Golf GTI is well, if not generously equipped. It lacks none of the essentials for a practical sporting car, but it leaves plenty of scope for additions to improve comfort and convenience and add that personal touch.

Standard fixtures and fittings have varied during the model's career, reflecting Volkswagen's pricing policy and the increasing competition in the 'hot hatch' market. For example, British-market Mark 1 GTIs were supplied on alloy wheels whereas in some other countries steel wheels were standard and the alloy rims optional. For the Mark 2, VAG (United Kingdom) Limited made Pirelli alloy wheels standard on the new five-door GTI, but a £420 option on the three-door. A steel sunroof was standardized on both Mark 2 variants, as were the driving lamps mounted in the grille; elsewhere, these are options.

So if you are buying secondhand it is worth checking the car's fittings, for the original owner may have paid quite a considerable sum on top of the 'book' price. It is also worth remembering that a car privately imported from the Continent may not have as high a specification as the equivalent model offered in the UK.

If you are buying new, consider the factory options list carefully; most are things that are difficult or very expensive to fit later. You will know if you like the idea of tinted glass and whether your kind of motoring would make a split rather than one-piece folding rear seat useful, so that you can carry a second passenger and bulky luggage. Electric windows look like an expensive option at nearly £400 — nearer £450 for the five-door — and can be very tiresome if they go wrong; not that the VW ones have a particularly bad record. On the other hand, central locking is a boon and quite reasonably priced. Headlamp washers are a useful safety item for muddy British winters and could well be worth the £120 or so charged.

The dealer, of course, can supply and fit a whole range of other items from the VAG parts list. Top of the list for cars not fitted with one as standard is a door mirror for the passenger side. It is a shortcoming of the Golf design that the mirrors are mounted too far back for optimum visibility, but it is still safer to have two rather than one.

A major after-market item that carries Volkswagen approval and does not affect the car's warranty is the tailor-made air conditioning system introduced in July 1985. This is made by Diavia and can be fitted to the GTI Mark 2 by Audi

Popular accessories for the Mark 1 GTI are this grille and spoiler incorporating supplementary lights. They are easily fitted, unlike the more elaborate components of body modification kits described in Chapter 6.

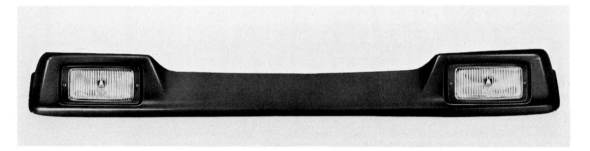

Volkswagen Air Conditioning Specialists. Price? Around £1,000....

We cover the many ways of personalizing your GTI with body kits and other exterior 'cosmetics' in Chapter 6, but a piece of mild customizing for GTI Mark 1s with a very practical purpose is to fit a four-headlamp grille. The headlamps of the Mark 1 are one of the few areas of criticism of the model. Improved lighting performance can be achieved by replacing the standard headlamp units with higher output ones such as Cibié Z180. More often, the standard 7-inch lamps are supplemented either by two $5\frac{3}{4}$-inch units, rather in the style of the Mark 2, or by another pair of 7-inchers, which requires a more elaborate grille (and different, shallower, lamps for the inner pair). Lighting specialists Hella — who also make Golf body kits — offer the first type of grille with either fog lamps or driving lamps. They also sell a spoiler kit incorporating two rectangular fog lamps.

You will see examples of other four-lamp fronts in Chapter 6; the replacement grilles can usually be obtained separately from the rest of the body kits. If you want to uprate the (improved) lighting of the Mark 2, Hella have chosen the GTI as the first application for their advanced DE light units. These are small and rectangular and have a tri-axial elipsoid reflector instead of the normal parabolic type and a separate internal lens instead of a conventional front lens; in effect, they project light on to the road. The full Hella Styling Kit

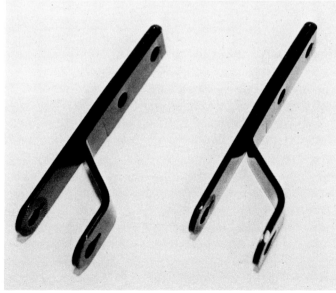

If you want fog lamps without the expense of special body parts to contain them, kits are available for underbumper mounting; this one is from Zender. GTi Engineering sell simple fog lamp brackets which bolt to the bumper irons and are suitable for several types of lamp.

includes two conventional H2 headlamps for main beam, two DE dipped-beam units alongside them and two DE fog lamps built into a special front spoiler. The spoiler with its little square DE lamps is available separately.

Now let's think about the inside of the GTI. Over the years the trim has ranged from tartan to simple cross-stripes. Retrimming is expensive if it is done

A sunroof is a desirable fitment, but installing a sliding steel roof, like that which is standard on the Mark 2 in the UK, is an expensive business in the after-market. The Volkswagen sliding roof does not have a very large aperture but a wind and noise deflector is included.

properly. Fancy leather? Tickford, the Aston Martin associates who specialize in high-quality special trimming, talk of £5,000 to give a Golf the full interior treatment: seats, facia, special headlining, Wilton carpet etc. Leather suppliers Connolly Brothers, of Wimbledon, South London, will retrim seats or doors if required; seats alone are likely to cost around £500.

Most owners are happy with VW's sports seats and so sales of those special but very expensive Recaros are slow to GTI owners. Fitting different seats brings up the problem of trim match again, though most are available in plain black and so merge quite well with the GTI's other fixtures. The standard sunroof in Mark 2s from January 1985 can make the headroom marginal for 6-foot-plus drivers. Other Golfs can have a rather crude seat height adjustment, but this is not available with the GTI's sports seats and in any case is intended to raise the seat for shorter drivers rather than lower its base. GTi Engineering will convert a Mark 2 seat and fit an adjuster to lower the base for around £185.

Fitting a different steering wheel is another way of 'tuning' the GTI driving position. There is a wide variety of special steering wheels on the market, many of which can be adapted for the Golf. Volkswagen Motorsport have a neat one with a stitched leather boss which is standard size; remember that fitting a smaller wheel may obscure the instruments and make the steering heavy to handle at parking speeds.

Early GTIs had a supplementary instrument panel in the centre console carrying an oil pressure gauge and a clock. Volkswagen's Votex accessory brand

There are lots of special steering wheels on the market. This neat leather-covered one, is available from Volkswagen Motorsport or Italvolanti (Dream Wheelers of Bedford) while more exclusive and much more expensive is the Treser wheel and polished wood gearlever knob from Thomson & Taylor of Cobham, Surrey.

offer a similarly useful panel for later models (available from GTi Engineering) for those who like to monitor the car's systems more thoroughly than the standard instruments, warning lights and computer read-out allow. Round black-faced VDO instruments fit neatly.

The centre console may also be used to instal more elaborate in-car

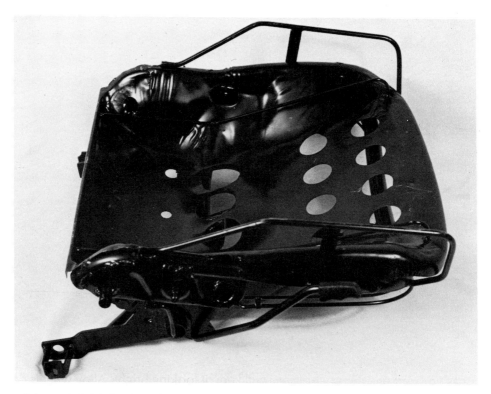

Tall drivers whose heads touch the roof of a Mark 2 Golf with a sunroof can be more comfortable if the seat is lowered. GTi Engineering will carry out a conversion which includes a height adjuster, but it isn't a simple job. A drivers seat with height adjustment is to become available from the factory in 1986.

entertainment equipment and some owners prefer to reposition the radio unit there instead of its highly visible mounting at the top of the facia. The choice of radio and cassette player and associated equipment is a matter of taste as well as cost. Volkswagen adopted a virtually vandal-proof rubber-covered spring aerial for the Mark 2, but it seems to give no better than average reception. The 16-valve model was shown at its announcement with a short, amplified aerial at the back of the roof, rather like that used on the Audi Avant estate; the distributor position of the new engine had apparently generated too much interference with a conventional front-mounted antenna.

Naturally, you want to keep your GTI in good condition. Tailor-made mats from VAG will preserve new carpets — or cover scruffy old ones. Mudflaps will not only help prevent following motorists being blinded by spray, but will also direct water and stones away from the sills and back of your car. Paintwork tends to get scratched and discoloured around the door handles and to protect against this VAG sell aluminium finger plates which fit into the recess behind the handle. Finished in matt black, they cost about £2.50 a pair.

Modern paintwork does not require any special treatment though regular

One solution to the problem of vandalized radio aerials is this rubber-covered spring antenna used by VAG on the Mark 2. It is said to be virtually indestructible, but a longer electrically retracting aerial would probably give similar security and better reception.

washing and proprietary polishes will keep it looking bright. Alloy wheels do, however, require some attention and brake dust can have an especially corrosive, discolouring effect on the front ones. When washing won't get them clean, use one of the special Alloy Wheel Cleaners available; we have had good results with the Lacro brand.

Roof racks are not desirable things from a noise, economy or aesthetic point-of-view, but you are not going to let wind-surfing or occasional removals stand in the way of Golf GTI ownership, are you? Mark 2 Golfs do not have conventional rain guttering, so the range of suitable roof racks is limited for these newer cars. Volkswagen dealers sell a Roof Carrying System made in Italy which consists of upright mountings to which various beams and frames can be fitted. The GTI's maximum roof load is 165lb.

Travelling abroad, local regulations may require you to carry a warning triangle and first-aid kit in the car, as well as spare light bulbs. A fire extinguisher is also a good precaution. So is some attention to security. Various alarm systems are available and it is worth the small cost of etching the car's registration number on the windows. It won't deter the joy-riding thief, but it makes it inconveniently difficult for the professional who would otherwise simply respray it and swap the number-plates for resale. An inevitable penalty of owning the most desirable small car in the business is that it is a magnet for thieves. So take precautions!

Keeping in shape

GRAHAM ROBSON is well-known to motoring enthusiasts as a contributor to several magazines and the author of over 50 motoring books. He specializes in automotive history, rallying (he was Standard-Triumph competition manager in the 1960s) and in carefully researched features on car buying, like the Buying Secondhand series in *Autocar*.

This GTI Mark 1 was kindly loaned for photography from the used car stock of Dovercourt at Battersea, London.

Graham Robson provides tips for getting the best out of your GTI — new or old

The most amazing feature of the GTI, when it was launched in 1975, was that it was so completely different from the old VW traditions. Not only was it much quicker than any previous model, but it was an entirely new character. In the old days, you bought a Beetle to keep slogging away for week after week, year after year — and the performance didn't matter at all. With the GTI, here was a car which could out-run any similar car in Europe, and out-handle it into the bargain.

To provide all this performance, and such inch-accurate handling, VW had to provide a more sophisticated chassis than ever before, and as the cars get older they deserve having quite a bit of time (and some money) lavished on them. Even though the Bosch fuel injection system and the electronic ignition (except on early examples) are almost free of maintenance requirements, it isn't wise to skimp on service.

Under normal circumstances, the GTI should be looked at by an official VW/ Audi dealer every 5,000 miles, or every six months if the mileage build-up is slow. Even if the owner is tempted to 'do his own thing' at the intermediate 5,000-mile intervals, he should certainly have a major check carried out every 10,000 miles, when items like the spark plugs, oil filter and other details are all changed. In fact quite a lot of owners have the plugs and filter changed every 5,000 miles.

It is worth noting — particularly if you intend to buy a secondhand example, and have not bargained for spending money on maintenance — that the 20,000-mile interval is *the* major one, for it involves the regular items, plus a check on all valve clearances (and reshimming the valve gear if necessary) and a change of brake fluid. As one service manager told me:

'Most owners don't like having the fluid changed, but we still recommend it, to make absolutely sure.....'

On the other hand, detail design, and life expectancy, of camshaft drive belts is now so high that there is no recommended swopping interval.

The first batch of GTIs to be delivered in the UK — from 1976 to summer 1979 — originally had left-hand drive. Many of these, in fact, have since been converted to right-hand drive — very professionally and very well — by GTi Engineering at Silverstone, and it is only an expert who can see how this was done. Even if you buy one of these cars, it will look, and feel, identical to a later RHD Golf GTI, and parts can, of course, be found to keep it in shape.

In this, and all other cases, it is as well to know what you expect to find before going 'shopping' for a used Golf GTI. After the original series of LHD cars were imported, the first official right-hand-drive models arrived in the summer of 1979. These cars had all the features later to become familiar to GTI lovers, but had the original type of all-synchromesh *four*-speed transmission, and 17.3mph/1,000rpm gearing. Even so, the top speed was about 110mph, at which the engine was turning over at 6,360rpm. But there weren't many of them, for the five-speed transmission (with 18.5mph/1,000rpm and a slightly higher top speed) was standardized from the autumn of 1979, and has been fitted to GTIs ever since then.

The other major change, introduced to the UK from September 1982, was that the engine size was enlarged, from 1,588cc to 1,780cc. The gearing was even higher than before (19.85mph/1,000rpm), and the top speed was up to

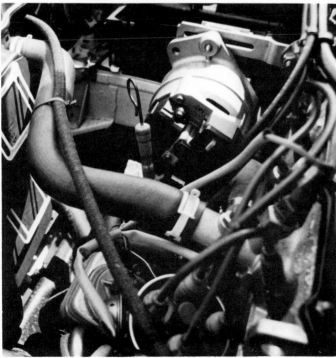

Plenty of space under the Mark 2 GTI bonnet, above, though fuel injection pipework has a long way to travel. Injection air flow sensor is in the moulded plastic chamber to the left. Ingenious flap valves behind radiator, left, alongside fan housing, regulate flow of air to underbonnet. Dipstick is conveniently located at front next to the alternator.

about 114mph, but the car was just as smooth, and just as delightful, as before. Finally, from the spring of 1984, came the rather larger Golf GTI Mark 2.

Accordingly, in the mid-1980s, the majority of all secondhand GTIs available in the UK are the five-speed Mark 1 variety, all of which have the three-door body style. From autumn 1981, incidentally, a five-door GTI was available, but only with left-hand drive, and it was never officially imported to the UK.

Once you have found your GTI what should you be doing to preserve it? First of all, try to keep it to the manufacturer's optimum settings, and don't fall for the glib claims of some specialists that their special tweaks, or components, can make a radical improvement. Usually they simply can't deliver what they promise.

Because the GTI was carefully developed by VW, whose engineers are among the most diligent in the world, it does not lack performance or roadholding. It's true that the roadholding can be further improved (at the expense of ride comfort — as we have already pointed out), but the standard car, as sold, is a satisfactory compromise.

It *is* worth ensuring, however, that the suspension settings are nominal — which is to say that the front wheels have $\frac{1}{4}$ degree negative camber, each side, and that there is between nil and 15 minutes toe-in to the front track. There is some slight adjustment to the front settings, to allow for this optimization. At the rear no adjustments are possible.

That camber setting, incidentally, may have been deranged by an earlier owner, if he has inadvertently gone 'kerbing' with the wheels on lock. There is nothing to be gained, though, in fiddling with tyre pressures — though perhaps a 2psi increase will give better steering precision, paid for by a slight loss in ride comfort.

Stick with factory settings of the engine, only deviating if you decide to fit a complete tuning kit. The Bosch injection is adjustment-free, in any case; NGK BP6ES or Champion N79Y plugs are as good as any other; and nominal factory valve clearances should be retained.

Use 4-star/97 RM octane fuel, and don't search around for additivies. Most owners find that there is nothing to be gained by using more than 6,000rpm, in any gear, and in any case you'll find that caning the engine gives the clutch a hard time. Normal engine operating levels are an oil pressure of 5-6 bar (and about 1 bar at idle), and an oil temperature of about 110 degrees C.

Tyres? There are many very good HR-rated radials these days. However, as with many other cars, the GTI is best driven on complete sets of covers, rather than a mixed bag. Some dealers recommend Pirelli P6 or Dunlop D4 tyres, but Michelin MX and Goodyear NCTs are also particularly suitable. You pay for enterprising cornering with wear — the fronts tend to wear out at least twice as quickly as the rears.

What will go wrong, as the cars get older? In summary — no more, and no

First right-hand drive GTIs mirrored left-hand drive predecessors, available only to special order, in having alloy-spoked sports steering wheel and 'golf ball' gearlever knob. Mark 2 left, follows pattern set by later Mark 1s, though switchgear is quite different.

less, than in other Golfs, except where the extra power has to be paid for. The engines are very sound, though eventually the valve oil seals deteriorate, oil finds its way down the guides, and the smokey-exhaust syndrome sets in; a relatively simple top overhaul usually restores the engine to health. For more serious cases, VAG exchange units are available — complete engine, 'short' motor, cylinder head and many other major components. The Bosch fuel injection system (as on so many other cars) seems to last indefinitely, so long as the fuel supply is kept water-free. Warm (as opposed to hot) start problems sometimes crop-up — and usually mean that one of the temperature sensors has gone on the blink.

GTI clutches have a hard time, especially before 1981 model-year changes saw an increased-diameter component fitted. Some owners, incidentally, must really have lost their temper with slipping clutches, for quite a few cars have suffered cables being punched through the passenger bulkheads!

Incidentally, don't buy a Golf and expect it to be completely silent mechanically. All GTIs, and particularly the new 16-valve variety, have an urgent whisper of mechanical 'clatter' (and that isn't meant to be an exaggeration) from the valve gear. Get used to it, and enjoy it — it's almost as accurate an indicator of the engine's speed as the rev-counter itself.

The good news about GTI body/monocoque units is that the model has been covered by a 6-year anti-corrosion warranty since March 1979 — which means, really, that almost every GTI sold in the UK is covered. To qualify for this cover, the car doesn't even need an annual inspection. However, the VW dealers I talked to remind that this only covers corrosion working its way *out*, from *inside* the metal — in other words, don't expect repairs to scrapes or stone damage to be covered.

GTIs eventually do rust, especially once they are beyond their third or fourth birthday, but it is a gradual process, and I have yet to see a car which would need work before it could face up to a British MoT test with equanimity. Naturally, the exhaust system develops holes, perhaps after the second birthday (sooner in areas where roads are heavily salted in winter), but the underpan in general doesn't seem to suffer.

On earlier cars, therefore, the rust has already started to appear, notably on the tops of the inner wheelarches, where the bolt-on front wings attach (you see this by opening up the bonnet and looking at each side of the engine bay), and around the headlamp cut-outs of the front wings.

'The usual places' is how one of my dealer acquaintances summed up the other 'where to look' points — which is to say on the sills under the doors (though cars fitted with mudflaps survive much longer), and on the clinched-over bottom edges of the doors, and the tailgate. The same source suggested that there are hardly ever any water leaks into a Golf GTI's cabin, though occasionally the rear lamp clusters let some in around their edges. If you are checking inside the boot compartment before buying a GTI, have a look at the

Luggage space with rear seats and parcels shelf in place is not over-generous in Mark 1 but adaptable. Spare wheel — full-size or 'spacesaver' — lives beneath the carpet and all the luggage has to be taken out to get at it!

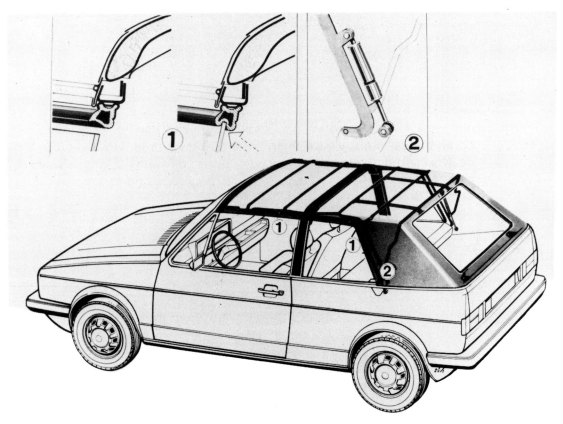

Golf Convertible's is a good hood — lined and with glass (and heated) rear window. It has a complicated frame, as this drawing shows, but this attention to detail gives saloon-like comfort when closed.

wheelarches which protrude into the space, for these sometimes suffer bangs and scratches from large loads thrown in over the quite high sill.

While you are looking over a GTI, before buying, perhaps, or at some time during ownership when you have time to analyse its condition, listen beyond the urgent engine noise for any rattles and dashboard vibrations. Look for signs of wear and noise at the suspension strut top mounts (they may 'clunk' when you bounce up over a kerb, for instance, if they are worn).

You shouldn't have any trouble with suspension ball-joints, and the rear end is so robust that dealers sometimes dispair of ever selling replacement parts for them!

The GTI, in fact, is the sort of car which most owners take pleasure in keeping right, and the design is such that, with regular service attention, it encourages this. Keep the suspension settings correct, the lubricant schedule up to date and the paintwork well cleaned, and it can be a joy for years.

Elements of a complete body kit. Mark 1 front (above) and Mark 2 rear (below) — these from Kamei — show what a difference cladding and decor can make to the GTI's appearance. Variations on all the components (right) are available from several manufacturers, as photographed in the following pages.

Notes of distinction

Ray Hutton reviews a selection of body parts and wheels to give your GTI that special look

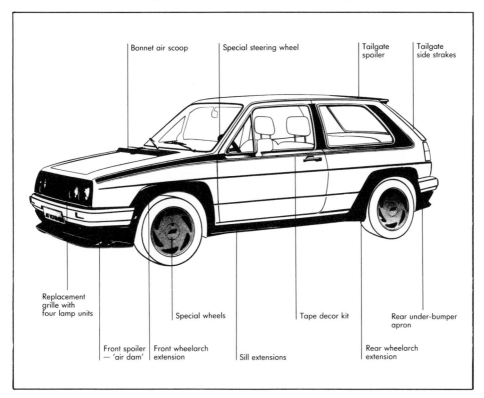

Bonnet air scoop | Special steering wheel | Tailgate spoiler | Tailgate side strakes

Replacement grille with four lamp units | Front spoiler — 'air dam' | Front wheelarch extension | Special wheels | Sill extensions | Tape decor kit | Rear wheelarch extension | Rear under-bumper apron

Since the Golf GTI first emerged from Wolfsburg a whole industry has grown up to supply the needs of enthusiastic owners. For every customer who admired the GTI for its lack of ornamentation and its subtle but distinctive red-line motif there was another who wanted it to look more what it actually is — a genuine high-performance car.

The GTI quickly became a cult car. Fashion brought even more popularity.

RAY HUTTON has followed the development of the GTI Cult from its early days. He was Editor of *Autocar* from the time of the car's inception until 1984. Now working as a freelance writer for the *Sunday Express Magazine*, *The Observer Magazine* and *TV Times*, as well as a number of motor trade and industry publications, Ray is also the editor of this MRP Enthusiast's Companion.

Body kit selection — two examples of converted Mark 2s from GTi Engineering — on the left, a Hella styling kit and, right, a full Zender kit including rear spoiler. Wheels on the Hella car are BBS, Zender version has that company's own wheels.

But, like the designer dress that gets sold in a chain store, numbers dilute the effect. To stand out from the in-crowd a GTI had to be more than the standard product. Special wheels would give it that distinctive touch. Colour-keying wheels and other brightwork would turn heads in Knightsbridge, let alone the local pub.

This up-market customizing wasn't just a British thing, extending the craze for wide-wheeled extended-arch Minis. The GTI's good news spread across the Continent and nowhere more so than in its home country. So most of the better equipment to personalize your GTI originates in Germany.

Body modifications available range from tape 'decor' kits to add an extra flash of colour and reflector panels spelling out 'Golf GTI' to complete sets of plastic cladding that can cost over £800 by the time they are fitted and painted. They cover the spectrum from discreet elegance to downright bad taste. But since they are a matter of taste, we will refrain from commenting on their individual appearance and concentrate on the practical matter of choosing and buying.

It is as well to clear up one thing at the outset. Whatever the makers may pretend, the prime function of these additional body items is appearance. They are most unlikely to show the slightest improvement in performance, stability or roadholding of a mechanically standard GTI. As has been said in Chapter 1, this was an engineer's car from the outset and has all it needs for optimum road performance. It has a front under-bumper air-dam bigger than an ordinary Golf's because it aided stability at high speed, but it doesn't have a rear spoiler because Wolfsburg's wind-tunnel tests showed that it didn't need one. The 16-

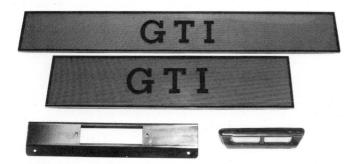

Simple customizing — tape 'decor kits' can give a different look without panel modification — these, top, from Kamei. Reflective rear panels, in different sizes for Mark 1 and Mark 2, left, come with kit to re-locate number-plate under bumper. Less polite name-plate, bottom, refers to US model.

*Putting on a new face —
alternative grille,
headlamp and front
spoiler treatments for
Mark 2. Top is from
Zender, with 2 H4 outer
dipping headlamps and
two inner main beam
units. Centre, Kamei
suggest 7in outer and
5¾ inner lamps with
distinctive intake.
Bottom is Oettinger
version with Hella DE
light units.*

Complete Hella body kit for GTI Mark 2 includes four DE headlamp unit as used by Oettinger, opposite, but with supplementary fog lamps of the same type in the under-bumper spoiler.

valve has a deeper air-dam than its predecessors and this has been adopted for production on all GTIs for the 1986 model year.

The bigger and more famous firms in this field all claim aerodynamic advantages and wind-tunnel 'optimization' of their body kits, but most are notably short of figures. True, Kamei do publish graphs showing reduced aerodynamic lift front and rear with their X1 kit, but most are couched in unspecified terms like 'improvement of drag coefficient'. So let's put this

Full X1 kit for Mark 1 from Kamei (UK agents Scotford of Bidford-on-Avon, Warwickshire) includes elaborate front spoiler and grille treatment plus side skirts.

Rear spoiler alternatives — Kamei version, right, can incorporate high level brake lights, while Hella version is deep enough to act as rain/ sun shield.

Hella's Mark 2 spoiler is more elaborate and claimed to reduce drag, but, significantly, the makers recommend fitting a passenger door mirror when the spoiler is in place!

Zender (GTi Engineering are the official UK agents) adopt a waist-level rear spoiler formed as part of a rear window surround. There is a cut-out for the wiper pivot but rear visibility is adversely affected.

Kamei X1 kits are available for both Mark 2 three-door, above, and five-door, below. Rear wheelarches cannot be modified so extensively on the five-door and there are other differences between the two kits, though overall visual effect is similar.

functional aspect on one side and say only that it must be advisable to go for a system that has been wind-tunnel tested because at least it should ensure that the add-ons will not ruin the aerodynamics of the original car. It is easy to do that by simply sticking too large a spoiler in the wrong place.

It is also worth noting that the Germans have strict standards for the safety of car accessories and that products which have their TUV certification should be of sound construction and safe from the point of view of other road users. Big spoilers with sharp edges can be dangerous and it was the Germans who led the way in the use of pliable materials for such items.

There was a time when this kind of body reshaping would have been the province of the specialist coachbuilder working in aluminium, hand-beaten and riveted into place. Today, the additional components are prefabricated in plastic. Most used to be glass-fibre, a material which the smaller companies and those at the cheaper end of the market still use as the production costs are low. Glass-fibre is a perfectly satisfactory material for car bodies, as Lotus and others will testify, but for add-on body parts more accurate mouldings in other plastics which can be better integrated with the metal are to be preferred.

ABS was widely used as a substitute for glass-fibre — and is still favourite for intricate grille panels and the like — but now the bigger parts of BBS and Zender kits are made from flexible polyurethane formed by RIM (Reaction Injection Moulding). The advantage of RIM is considerable since it can cope with light

BBS body kits are handled by the Kitz Group, a division of VAG (United Kingdom) Ltd. This one, for the Mark 2 GTI, has deep front spoiler wheelarch extensions, side sills, rear apron and RS three-piece modular alloy wheels.

Mark 1 GTI with Zender body kit and rectangular lamp grille, all red apart from screen pillars and rear spoiler. Wheels are ATS. Neat registration 'A12' identifies this as the property of John Atkins of Jamesigns, the number-plate brokers.

impacts by deforming and returning to its original shape. It is the same material as used for the 'soft' bumpers of cars like the Porsche 928. ABS is prone to crack even after a light knock and can't be repaired satisfactorily.

Spoilers, particularly those for rear mounting, are usually formed from semi-rigid polyurethane foam and have both the consistency and appearance of hard rubber.

The expense of tooling for RIM is part of the reason for the relatively high price of the top-class kits. But specialist retailers who deal in Golf body parts at a range of prices — as many of them do — point out that the products of BBS, Hella, Kamei and Zender, for examples, fit well and produce a better final finish than their cheaper imitators.

In fact, one specialist told us that 'dimensions of the cars vary more than the body kits' for inevitably even robot-welded bodyshells vary from side to side and from one to another by a few millimetres. This is one of the reasons why fitting the more comprehensive body kits is not a job for the average do-it-yourselfer.

The professionals pre-fit the components, fettling them for their precise location. They are then painted off the car before being fitted, usually by a combination of screws and bonding (the latter with a 'two pack' adhesive).

BBS offer two versions of their Mark 1 Golf body kit. Above is the 'Round' kit with curved wheelarch extensions; the alternative is the more angular 'Square'. Below is a 'full house' Zender body conversion for a Mark 1 with 7in wide wheels, necessitating cutting away the original wheelarches. Note the four 7in headlamps on this car.

Most GTI body kits originate in Germany. These are exceptions. Top is a Mark 2 kit made in ABS by Bubble Car in Italy and sold in the UK by Dream Wheelers of Bedford. Centre is a British kit from Kat Designs of Hanslope, Bucks, using glass-fibre panels. Bottom is an unusual style from Orciari in Italy (British agents, Italtune Ltd of Macleod Street, London SE17) which uses glass-fibre panels and an ABS grille with electrically-operated sliding hatches to reveal lamps.

Perhaps the wildest of all is this Mark 1 Golf with a touch of the DeLoreans — it was produced by the Swiss tuning firm Rinspeed, who are better known for their Porsche conversions. Gull-wing doors need plenty of height in the garage and presented a snag — when you are sitting inside you can't reach the handles to close them...

Painting is tricky as not only does an exact match have to be made with the body colour, but the characteristics of the material must be considered. Some plastics are very solvent-sensitive, while others, designed to be flexible in use, need a higher proportion of plasticizers in the paint than the rigid ones. Most body kit parts are supplied in primer, but the specialist fitters like GTi Engineering tend not to rely on the consistency of manufacturers' paint samples and mix their own, knowing from experience how to shade to match the original painted steel.

Painting all brightwork and exterior trim — metal or plastic — in body colour has been increasingly popular, but it has to be said it is much more successful in some colours than others.

Rear spoilers usually come in black and can either be finished in body colour or left unpainted. Most are relatively simple to fit with a few screws and double-sided adhesive tape; the manufacturers supply templates for correct location. At least one type is simply bonded to the tailgate.

Front spoilers and front and rear bumper aprons are more complicated. Some, like the Zender Z20, fit over the standard bumpers, but only after their plastic cladding has been removed, while others mount below the bumpers or replace them altogether.

We have already touched on the lighting improvements that can be achieved by using different or double light units on a Mark 1. Of all the body kit components, the 'face' — the grille and lamp arrangement — is probably the one that has the most dramatic visual effect. Round or rectangular lamps, large

Golf Convertible can use many of the styling parts for the hatchback, as Bubble Car conversion, above, shows. Note also the special Italian wheels. Kamei have created what Volkswagen have not, to date — a Mark 2 Convertible, right. Called the X1-Speedster, it also differs from the original in not having a central hood-supporting roll-over hoop and the hood concealed when retracted beneath a rear deck panel.

or small; there's a wide choice.

Obviously the kit makers would like to sell a complete set of their equipment, but the discerning GTI customizer will often pick between two or more suppliers to produce his or her individual look. It is not at all unusual to choose a grille and lamp cluster from one supplier and wheelarches, front spoiler and sill panels from another. But take care that the chosen panels complement each other if they join. Remember, too, that not much that was designed for the Mark 1 Golf is applicable to the Mark 2, though by subtle reshaping some of the manufacturers have managed to achieve a similar effect with their kits for the two cars.

The other ever-popular piece of customizing that has a major effect on appearance is special wheels. Again, the choice is enormous and so is the range of prices — from about £30 to over £200 each. Changing wheels is an expensive business for it is usual to go up in width and possibly wheel diameter

BBS REWRITE THE STORY OF THE WHEEL.
IN THREE PARTS.

This is the BBS RS 3-part wheel.

As you can see from the illustration below, it has a split rim, so it weighs considerably less than ordinary alloy wheels. True to form it also runs far, far more precisely.

The RS wheel is not only built to the most exacting standards possible, it's also built to BBS standards.

So high are these, we insist on making all 32 bolts on the wheel ourselves.

We then drive it more than 1200 miles, carrying two and a half times the normal wheel load.

We simulate cornering 800,000 times at high speed. To gain the much prized but seldom awarded TÜV approval from the German government we need

only have done so 200,000 times.

We then spray salt for 300 hours to be sure every wheel will resist corrosion. We even X-ray the centre looking for the minutest flaw. Finally, we give every wheel a two year guarantee.

Not surprisingly, the RS wheel is the only 3-part wheel to achieve TÜV approval.

From £200 a rim, it's not only the best road wheel in the world, it's also the most expensive.

If it's any consolation, we spared no expense building it. (This is true of every wheel we build, even our very much less expensive range of standard alloy wheels.) As any Volkswagen dealer will only too readily tell you.

WITH BBS YOU'RE OUT ON YOUR OWN

BBS WHEELS AND AERODYNAMIC COMPONENTS FOR VOLKSWAGEN AND OTHER FINE MARQUES.

Above: VW adopted Pirelli's 'Plus One' concept for the last 'campaign' Mark 1 GTIs which used these distinctive Pirelli alloy wheels in 14in diameter with 60-series tyres. The same 185/60 Pirelli P6 tyres are used on the Mark 2, with the alloy wheels standard on the five-door, optional on the three-door.

Right: Classic alloy wheel from BBS is one of several patterns from this company and popular fitment for the GTI.

Some of the many alloy wheel variations available: racing-style three-part BBS wheel is 20 per cent lighter but significantly more expensive than one-piece cast wheel; another BBS pattern (below left); Audi Quattro-like Ronal (below right); two of a wide range from ATS (bottom row).

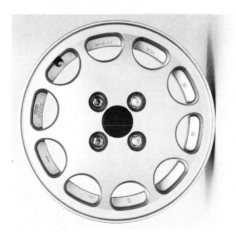

(to use a lower-profile tyre) so that one has to consider the cost of four, possibly five, wheels and tyres — at least £120 a go, averaging perhaps £180. It's not hard to spend £1,000 on a set of new 'boots' — and since the discarded ones won't be worth much unless they are brand new it is probably a good idea to plan the switch when the original tyres are wearing out....

There can be good justification for fitting wider and lower-profile tyres in terms of improved roadholding but, again, there are trade-offs, in ride and/or in steering heaviness. The standard Volkswagen set-up for the Mark 2 GTI — 6in wide, 14in diameter rims with 185/60-series tyres — is probably the best compromise for the normal engine output. Those who value grip above all will like the look of ultra-low profile 'supertyres' like the Pirelli P7 on 15in diameter wheels, but they will find the ride harsh and noisy.

Tyre technology continues to develop and by present-day standards the original 1977 Golf GTIs were somewhat under-tyred on their 175/70-13s on 5½in rims. A popular conversion was to 185/60-series tyres on 6in wide, 14in diameter wheels — what Pirelli called the 'Plus One' concept. In Britain, Volkswagen adopted this size and Pirelli's own distinctive alloy wheels for the Special Edition that marked the end of the Mark 1 GTI. The same combination became standard for the Mark 2, though the alloy rims were made an option for the main-selling three-door model.

Those wanting to go further with the Mark 2 tend to 15in diameter, 6 or 7in wide. Such a low-profile set-up can also be used on the Mark 1, but 7in rims require generous wheelarch extensions and some cutting away of the original bodywork for clearance.

Which ones to choose? There are over a dozen different suppliers of alloy wheels suitable for the Golf and some of them have 20 or more different designs! The choice will depend on price and appearance mostly, but it is important to make sure that the wheel *is* the right type in terms of inset and wheel nut location and type. Quality is important — and tends to be proportional to price — and there is reassurance in one of the four international safety standards — BS AU50 Part 2, TUV (Germany), JWL (Japan) and SEMA 5.1A (USA).

Bearing in mind the investment involved, it is a good idea to consider one of the wheel patterns that incorporates a lockable hubcap (a number of the ATS wheels have this feature) or to fit one lockable nut to each wheel.

It is not just a question of selecting a wheel design, either. These days they come in different colours from clear lacquered polished metal to black, gold and stove enamel in body colours. And for that 'all over' look, wheels can be painted by specialists with the right equipment using modern two-pack paints. Matching enhanced bodywork and wheels is a fashionable effect. Next step — coloured tyres?

One day you'll settle down with a roof over your head.

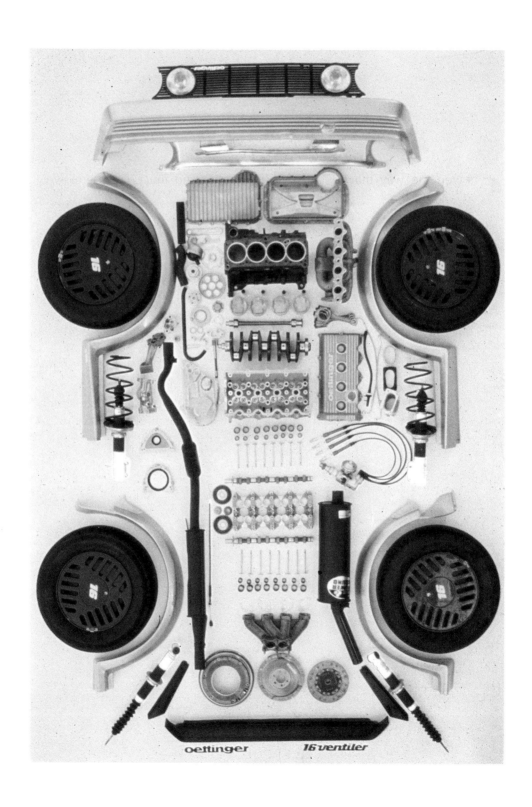

Quick car, quicker still

GTI conversions for even greater performance investigated by Jeremy Walton

Given the way that the factory have improved the GTI progressively through four versions, it is clear that making this VW go quicker still has become harder model-by-model.

For the original 110bhp 1600 and 112 horsepower 1800s, improved braking was a greater priority than more engine power. All that is attended to on the current 1800, and there can be very few owners with any serious gripes on the all-round performance of a GTI 16-valve. Human nature being unable to ignore a challenge, there will be plenty of modifications offered to cover even the 130mph 16V. But think seriously about the cost, refinement and possible mpg penalties before tackling any conversion.

For example, many of the turbocharging conversions offered for the GTI will knock a hole in the wonderful spread of both torque and power, as well as ruining the fuel consumption. The same applies to the more radical 16-valve and big-capacity engine conversions. Think very carefully about genuinely improving the GTI to suit your life-style *before* hacking about the product of millions of Deutschmarks spent on R&D at Wolfsburg!

Having an earlier-model GTI is a definite plus in the conversion game, because there is so much you can do that is irrelevant on the current-shape car. For example, VW put in a bigger fuel tank as part of the GTI Mark 2 deal, along with four-wheel disc brakes and the standard fitment of 60-series tyres — which had been optional in most markets outside Britain. Therefore, if you have an original 1600 GTI, the first steps of a sane owner would be to uprate the chassis performance before that smoothly injected 1.6 takes a power boost.

The broadest spread of UK equipment and advice comes from Richard Lloyd's aptly-titled GTi Engineering at Silverstone Circuit, Towcester, Northants. However, don't talk to them about turbocharging, because they have studiously ignored it for the 300 complete customer engine conversions they had delivered by June 1985. And don't expect them to be cheap....

Left: The works — Oettinger's complete conversion kit for a GTI 1800 includes their 16-valve cylinder head that preceded the factory's 16V. Power output for the Mark 1 1800 conversion is 142bhp.

JEREMY WALTON probably has more experience of tuned and modified cars than any writer in Britain. They have been a special interest for him since his early journalistic work at Cars & Car Conversions and Motoring News in the 1960s and early 1970s. He writes for those two magazines today, as well as many others, in particular Motor Sport and Performance Car. Also the author of several books including MRP's XR: The Performance Fords.

GTi Engineering's modified Mark 1 GTI on the company's rolling road dynamometer at Silverstone.

Given our hypothetical standard-spec 1600 GTI, the mixed disc/drum brake system can be uprated via simple pad and shoe material substitutes, and the sometimes sloppy RHD transfer linkage of earlier cars can also be improved. Good results have been reported for the grooved Tar-Ox discs and pads from Italtune. After that you may consider fitment of larger, vented front discs with appropriate calipers, but this — as with trying to imitate the factory four-wheel disc layout of the Mark 2 — is getting towards such large labour and parts bills that changing the car might be more realistic.

As with anything in mechanical life, it is possible to uprate the 1.6 braking system to give fully satisfactory results, but even some of the big disc conversions I have tried on the road have had excessive pedal 'slop' because the master cylinders had not been uprated, or were matched incorrectly to the new equipment.

If you fancy a bigger fuel tank in the original body, GTI do a 9-gallon unit that fits into the standard spare-wheel well of the Mark 1.

Most 1.6 owners with an eye to a conversion will be looking for more power. The simplest method is to imitate VW and go for 1.8 litres with a modest horsepower boost and plenty of mid-range torque.

GTi Engineering used to expand the 1.6 to 1.8 litres using the original flat cylinder head with Heron-headed pistons, a principle VW dropped when they went from 79.5mm x 80mm [1,588cc] to 81mm x 86.4mm [1,781cc] for the current eight and 16-valve engines.

In 1985 GTi still offered two 1.6-to-1.8-litre conversions: RLR 1800, rated at 130bhp, and RLR 1800 Plus, for another 10 horsepower. As for all their engine capacity conversions, the heart of the matter is a forged steel crankshaft, available with VW-style 86.4mm or a bonus long-throw 94.5mm stroke. Until 1984, a further crank throw of 90.5mm was available from GTi, but it was dropped as it was discovered to be a source of vibrations in later 2-litre conversions.

One could pick a standard VW 1800 stroke of 86.4mm and combine it with 81mm forged Cosworth pistons for the usual 1,781cc — but of very much

Heart of GTi Engineering's various engine modifications is a cylinder head with gas-flowed ports, and matched inlet manifold, larger valves, heavy-duty springs and high-lift camshaft. The head is available in this form or as part of an exchange engine deal.

Going faster, for longer in a modified Mark 1? This long-range auxillary fuel tank from GTi Engineering fits in the spare-wheel well to give an extra nine gallons. It fills through the existing filler neck and uses the original tank gauge.

stronger componentry in the GTi-supplied version.

If you already have an 1800, whether in the original body or the current shape, GTi Engineering offer a wide range of modifications. Most popular is the Plus Pac, at about £1,000 including VAT and fitting in Britain. The 23bhp bonus is extracted via a new 276-degree duration camshaft and a gas-flowed cylinder head carrying replacement, larger diameter, inlet and exhaust valves. Also replaced is the exhaust manifold, whilst both injection and distributor are modified.

That 1800PP is rated at 135bhp, developed some 400rpm further up the tachometer scale than standard. The even more comprehensive RLR 2000 Plus promises 150 horsepower, comfortably more than even the factory 16V! A 2-litre conversion comprises Cosworth forged 82.5mm pistons allied to the long-throw crank of 94.5mm for a capacity of 2,021cc.

Although I have reservations about 150 horsepower in a roadgoing GTI, there are plenty of people prepared to give you that, and more, amongst the turbo and continental tuning fraternity. For instance, Geoff Kershaw's Turbo Technics concern at 17 Galowhill Rd, Brackmills, Northampton NN4 0EE, offered exactly 150bhp for £1,782.50 including UK VAT during 1985.

Turbo Technics concentrated on building up a Garrett AiResearch T3 turbocharger in alliance with a replacement high nickel iron exhaust manifold

We will make your Golf GTi everything that you want it to be

BREATHTAKING PERFORMANCE!
Just imagine what 20% more power would do for your Golf GTi— the Q-Car of the '80s. Our **Plus Pac Conversion** raises power output from 112 bhp to 135 bhp.

Abundant reports in the Motoring Press praise it for its **performance, reliability and economy.** Fitting takes two to three days and during this time we'll keep you mobile with one of our courtesy cars!

For the technically minded, an extensively re-worked cylinder head and valve gear is the key to this exhilarating power increase, coupled with a specially designed camshaft, modified exhaust and inlet manifolds and a re-worked distributor, all developed from years of experience in building race-winning Golf engines.

Other Golf GTi (1 & 2) engine conversions include:
- 2 litre 8-valve 152 bhp Conversion giving 37% extra power
- 2 litre 16-valve 170 bhp Oettinger Conversion, giving 52% extra power

LIMPET-LIKE ROADHOLDING!
"Straightline stability is as good as the standard car but its response to direction changes is in a different league."

"At very high speed the car can be pointed at will with confidence…"
CARS & CAR CONVERSIONS

Our **Sports Suspension kit**, giving a firmer ride and lower ride height, is responsible for these enthusiastic comments. Alternatively, we can just lower the ride height

which keeps the centre of gravity low and still gives your GTi that road-hugging look. Our **Suspension Braces** complete the suspension package (essential for competition use).

Reassuringly, our **Brake Pad Conversion** helps *"kill any traces of fade during heavy applications",* says Cars & Car Conversions.

WHEELS & TYRES
Combinations of BBS, ATS, Ronal and Zender wheels, with Pirelli, Goodyear, Uniroyal and Dunlop tyres, are available from stock, but we do suggest that you seek our advice on the various dos and don'ts. A very important aspect of your car in terms of both appearance and handling.

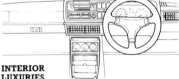

INTERIOR LUXURIES,
Feel the luxury of our choice of real leather 'GTi Engineering' embossed 14" **Steering Wheels** (black, white, red or blue).

Make parking child's play with our **Power Steering Conversion** (especially for cars fitted with wide wheel/tyre combinations) developed from VW components. Keep an eye on temperatures and pressures with **VDO Gauges** mounted in the integrally designed **Console Panel.** Reach for a cassette, stored in the **Cassette Holder** compartment with closable front, and keep a cool head with an **Air Conditioning System.**

We also supply and fit: ● Granadaphone Carphones ● ICE installations ● Security Alarms ● VDO Cruise Controls ● Leather Interiors ● Floor Mats

HEAD-TURNING BODY STYLING
A great opportunity for self-expression! We've got BBS, Zender, Bubble Car, Hella and Kamei kits, plus front and rear spoilers, wheel arches, sill panels, grilles etc., to choose from. And we'll finish them off with the very best in paint jobs in our advanced 'low-bake' spray booth facility.

Driving position too high?
We've got a modification which lowers the seat base. Height adjustment can then be made using a lever at the front of the seat. (Also available for passengers' seats.)

SERVICING, TOO! Don't forget that we also undertake regular servicing of all Audi Volkswagens. Our up-to-the-minute equipment (including a Rolling Road) and willing staff ensure that we'll get it right for you.

Photo shows:
Zender Z6 Body Kit, Zender Rear Wing, BBS 7 x 15 Modular Alloy Wheels, Pirelli P7 tyres.

Certain Body Kits and Wheels are not on the Approved List of Audi Volkswagen Accessories.

Illustrations are Copyright and may not be reproduced. All prices shown are subject to VAT.

GTi ENGINEERING

GTi Engineering Limited, Silverstone Circuit, Towcester, Northants NN12 8TN. Telex: 317447

Telephone: (0327) 857857

V·A·G **Audi** **VW**

Official Audi Volkswagen Conversion Specialists.

Please phone for intelligent and helpful answers to your queries and a free data sheet on Engine Conversions. Alternatively, send £1 for your Information Pack and Price List on the full Audi Volkswagen range of conversions.

VISA

The most comprehensive range of genuine Audi Volkswagen/VAG spares is available over the counter or by Mail Order to the UK and Overseas.

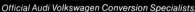

and front-mounted intercooler. They lowered the compression to 9.3:1 and tapered maximum boost carefully, boosting to 0.57bar for maximum torque around 3,000 revs, but letting the turbocharged effect droop slightly to 0.50bar at 6,000rpm. This was a sensible precaution and you will find similar principles applied to Ford's production RS Turbo Escort, which has been widely praised for its civility.

There are plenty of other turbocharger concerns in the UK; Janspeed, at Castle Rd, Salisbury, Wilts SP1 3SQ, are probably the best known. GTi Engineering also tried another interesting tack that preserved, nay enhanced, every ounce of mid-range torque pound-footage, for their application of a mechanical Roots supercharger, an American Magnacharger, yielded a shattering 165bhp and 150lbft torque from a standard 1800 unit!

Motor commented of it: 'With power increased 47% and torque up by 37% this Golf GTI tops 130mph — but don't ask about the fuel consumption.' That summed up why GTi Engineering did not go into production; besides, they were already working on 170bhp versions of a 16-valve Golf!

Taking the international view, the most famous and well-accepted of the GTI modification specialists has been Dipl-Ing Gerhard Oettinger & Co KG, of Max-Planck Strasse 36, 6382 Friedrichsdorf, West Germany. In 1977 they presented their first prototype 16-valve GTI engine, this 1.6-litre becoming available two years and the best part of 2 million Deutschmarks later.

Those development costs began to be amortized when VW decided to test-market the 16-valve's appeal via VW in France, who needed something to fight the Renault 5 Turbo. Originally VW had planned, and produced in a small initial batch, a turbocharged version of their four-cylinder engine; so far as I know, this was to be launched in the Scirocco, but a factory fire, worries about fuel consumption, and the recession aborted the project.

Thus the Oettinger 16V motor, which consisted of a new alloy head running a 10.5:1 compression fitted to the otherwise standard 1,588cc engine, went on sale in France as the VW Golf 16S ('S' for *Soupapes*). Such engines were rated 26bhp beyond the standard 1.6, giving a maximum figure of 136bhp at 6,500rpm. *Auto Hebdo*, the French/Belgian weekly enthusiast magazine, recorded 0-62mph in 8.9 seconds, a maximum of 124mph and rather poor fuel consumption that equated to 23.5mpg.

Although several thousand Oettinger 16-valve Golfs were sold on the Continent, senior VW engineers were not over-impressed with their reliability. When it came to doing their own engine there were fundamental differences — some of which they were forced into when they suffered their own share of teething troubles.

However, the Oettinger 16-valve conversion was extremely successfully applied to the 1800 GTI. *Auto Motor und Sport* recorded 7.7sec for 0-62mph, a 128.5mph maximum and a far more creditable 29.1mpg, very slightly less than their figure for a standard 1800 in the original body. These figures, taken three years before the factory 16V was available, were a tremendously accurate prediction of the performance VW would offer. Oettinger claimed a believable 142bhp at 6,100rpm, with the assistance of a cylinder head giving a slightly lower 10.2:1 compression ratio.

Distinctive underbonnet appearance of Oettinger twin-cam 16-valve engines for GTI Mark 1, left, and Mark 2. Mark 1 Oettinger engines develop between 136bhp and 160bhp, depending on capacity, 1.6 to 2 litres. Mark 2 E/16 engines are rated at 150bhp for the 1.8 and 170bhp for the 2-litre.

In action — Oettinger's 16-valve 1800 Mark 1 on the road. An earlier 1.6-litre version was sold as a mainstream model by Volkswagen in France.

That was far from the end of Oettinger's conventional aspirations for the VW 'four'. Utilizing a slight overbore, and a long-stroke steel crank [81.5mm x 94.5mm] for 1,972cc, they installed the 16-valve head once more. A lot of companies tried this recipe, including, in Britain, GTi Engineering, at Silverstone, and the Ted Toleman-owned VW dealership of Edwards, at Tamworth, Worcestershire.

Motor Sport's correspondent Alan Henry was able to try the extensively modified GTI with a Toleman link and reported a 0-60mph time in the region of 7.1 seconds and a top speed of just over 135mph. Coupled to an average of 26.4mpg throughout his test, AH was impressed enough to write, 'the intention has been to combine sheer performance and the sort of flexibility synonymous with the standard VW GTI power unit. Our feeling is that they have succeeded extremely well'.

This Oettinger 2.0 GTI was fitted with many other modifications, including a clutch-type limited-slip differential. It was obvious that my former colleague did not like the strange snatching and twitching engendered by LSD and high powered front-wheel drive any more than I would have anticipated! Even back in April 1982, when that report appeared, the engine cost nearly £3,000....

Apart from the engine, there is still much you can do to a GTI. First, the

Turbo Technics fitted a Garrett AiResearch T3 turbocharger to this otherwise innocent looking Mark 2 GTI to give a power boost to 150bhp, 0-60mph acceleration in 7 seconds, and a maximum speed of around 125mph. Underbonnet, left, shows little evidence of the turbo, but needs careful attention to cooling and includes a charge air intercooler.

unglamorous task of uprating the transmission. Outputs much beyond the 130-135bhp level seem to demand a stronger clutch, and it is noticeable that such a component is part of Turbo Technics' 150bhp conversion. VW Motorsport in Hannover (via GTi Engineering for Britain) are more interested in race and rally competitors and price their products accordingly. A close-ratio gear set costs about £600 in the UK; a limited-slip differential, an additional £444. There is also a wide choice of final-drive ratios, priced a little beyond £200.

Needless to say, VW Motorsport can supply all the hardware needed to compete with a Golf, particularly in Group A, where they have enjoyed notable class rallying success. Club racers in Britain can also get first-hand know-how from the proprietor of Autocavan, 103 Lower Weybourne Lane, Bagshot Lea, Farnham, Surrey. Geoff Thomas has developed one Golf since 1976, through stages as diverse as turbocharging to 200bhp club racer, winning the *Motor* accolade for '1978 Tuned Car of the Year.'

I drove the Autocavan Golf racer in 1,813cc [81mm x 88mm] capacity, with twin 48 DCOE Weber carburettors and a 7,400rpm limit. Weighing only 650kg with skimpy bodywork and no more interior trim than a single racing seat, this car proved frighteningly effective.

It overcame a back-of-the-grid Brands Hatch practice placing, actually passing 14 cars to finish second in class, fifth overall, after lapping within a second of a new 80mph lap record with a stranger at the wheel. I reckon Geoff Thomas knows a bit about quick VW motoring, and I know Autocavan are set up to cater for the less well-heeled owner with prices that will particularly appeal to those struggling to run secondhand GTIs.

Bilstein were the original damper suppliers for the GTI and their kit to uprate the car's suspension has VW's blessing. Uprated springs usually go hand in hand with improved wheels and tyres — in this case BBS 'classic' alloy 6J with Pirelli P7.

Although I feel that a limited-slip differential is best reserved for smooth race tracks, there are plenty of suspension tricks to be played that will enhance the handling of the road car. Personally, I reckon 140 horsepower is a maximum for the road, because that is the comfortable front-drive limit of the production GTI; the factory's 139bhp 16V gives you a clue on that!

The three principal contenders for your roadgoing expenditure are suspension kits from Sachs and Bilstein in West Germany, plus the Dutch Koni dampers. The Bilsteins are available in a Sport Pack of springs and dampers which comes complete with every little item needed to fit them, plus rear bushes to isolate any extra harshness. A typical GTi Engineering price for the Bilstein pack in 1985 was £412, with Sachs at £362. Konis were sold at £295 from companies such as Demon Tweeks, at Dept 5, High St, Tattenhall, Nr Chester, Cheshire CH3 9PX — again complete with front and rear coil springs.

Which is best? There was no doubt in my mind that Bilstein had done the job correctly and I was not surprised to learn that they were the only suspension conversion approved by the factory. Yet the development work in Germany did not provide the best British bumpy B-road ride. The same went for Koni, leaving

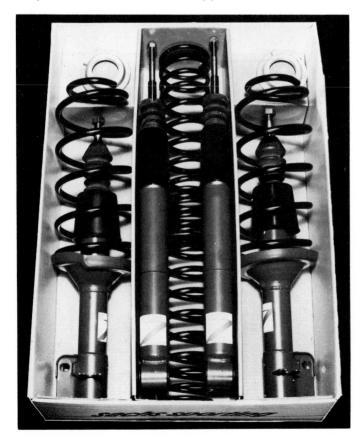

As they come — the Sachs GTI suspension kit that impressed Jeremy Walton is supplied with front struts, rear shock absorbers, special springs and bushes.

Novel way of illustrating Koni's suspension kit clearly shows progressive-rate rear springs with tighter coiling at their base than at the top.

Sachs as the correct compromise for UK road use, for they retain reasonable ride comfort. If smooth road speed is the sole aim, then go with Bilstein.

Tyres? Most of the performance Golfs I have tried have been on the 185/60 Pirelli P6, and I see little reason to change, save to warn against their aquaplaning traits, even when the tread looks healthy. Pirelli are aware of the problem, and they have produced the P600 in the same sizes for eventual Golf fitment — or you can go to the expense of P7s on rims up to 7 inches wide. This will not overcome the flights over deep puddles, but the sheer grip under any other condition is worth experiencing..... if you can afford it!

Of the alternative tyres available, Goodyear NCTs or BF Goodrich are likely to offer good grip, along with MXV from Michelin. In my view, the edge goes to P6 Pirelli for combining quiet running, some ride quality and sheer grip that ends in a controllable slide; some of the other choices can make the handling a bit 'sudden', or promote a harshness that is not part of a good roadgoing Golf. In case it sounds as if Pirelli are paying me I would add that I pay for either Goodyear or Uniroyal on my own cars, but that is because I feel they are best suited to those particular models. Horses for courses.....

Fitting wider wheels and low-profile tyres can make steering that is already on the heavy side at parking speeds unmanageably so. The 16V was the first GTI with power-assisted steering, but this became an option for the regular car in the 1986 model year. GTi Engineering offer an expensive — £1,200-plus — power steering conversion for older Mark 2s, with the added advantage of a higher ratio, 3.25 turns from lock to lock compared with 3.75 for the standard unassisted system.

Convenient or not, in the eyes of many enthusiasts, adding power steering is taking the 'softening' of the GTI too far. Why, they will be fitting automatic transmission next..... The factory have no plans for that, but GTi Engineering will once again come to the rescue if you must have an automatic GTI and can afford around £2,000 for the conversion.

FURTHER INFORMATION FROM VOLKSWAGEN SALES ENQUIRIES, YEOMANS DRIVE, BLAKELANDS, MILTON KEYNES, MK14 5AN. TELEPHONE: (0908) 679121. EXPORT AND FLEET SALES, 95 BAKER STREET, LONDON W1M 1FB. TELEPHONE: 01-486 8411.

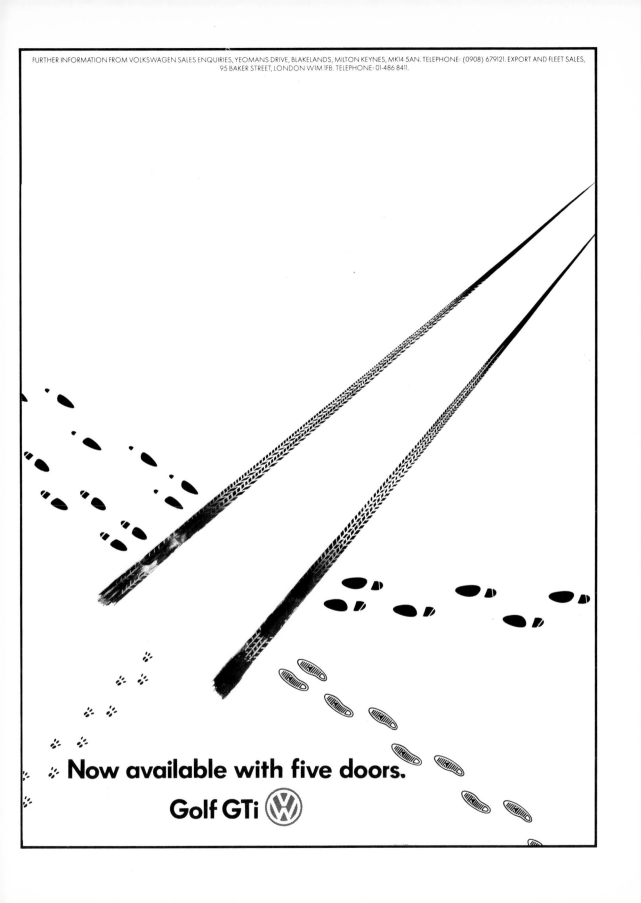

Now available with five doors.

Golf GTi

Facing the competition

The GTI wasn't built to race or rally but turned out to be an ace, as Peter Newton explains

Volkswagen were mindful of motor sport when the GTI was first produced — they planned to make 5,000 to meet the Group 1 Production Saloon regulations in force at the time — but competition has never played a major part in the marketing of the high-performance Golf. So it is easy to overlook the considerable success that the model has enjoyed in rallies and on the race track; the achievements have been in the less glamorous mass production-based categories and more often class rather than outright wins.

The GTI's motor sport career can be traced back to 1974 — long before the car was announced — when the VW Motorsport department at Hannover created a 1,500cc Group 1 Golf for Freddy Kottulinsky to drive (Kottulinsky, a notable, if at times unrestrained, Formula 3 driver, would later play an important role in the development of the Audi Quattro).

VW Motorsport had hitherto been involved almost exclusively with the administration of worldwide Formula Super Vee single-seater racing. At that time, and still today, the department was presided over by the elegant Klaus Peter Rosorius, a tall, gaunt, sad-eyed Austrian with a throw-away humour as dry as a Salt Lake City liquor mart.

Rosorius joined Volkswagen from Continental Tyres in 1972. VW's competition history goes back to 1965 and the importation from the United States of 10 1,200cc Beetle-engined Formula Vee racing cars by Porsche. Formula Vee and its more powerful successor Super Vee was an important training ground for some of today's racing stars, among them 1982 World Champion Keke Rosberg, who won the Super Vee title in 1975.

Super Vee transferred from the air-cooled Beetle engine to the water-cooled Golf and became increasingly sophisticated. A natural development was to adapt the GTI engine to Formula 3, which calls for the use of production-based engines up to 2 litres with an air inlet restrictor designed to limit power and produce evenly competitive racing. Today, British preparation specialist John

PETER NEWTON is the editor of the monthly magazine *Cars & Car Conversions* and has a long and deep interest in rallying, as a participant and as a reporter. He was rallies editor of *Autosport* before joining 'Triple C'. He has followed the progress of the Volkswagen Motorsport department through the GTI's career and knows the drivers who have brought the car such success in international events.

Right: Kalle Grundel has been Volkswagen Motorsport's GTI rally star, achieving some remarkable results in the Group A category, starting with a Mark 1 1800 in 1983.

Judd works closely with VW Motorsport, for whom Formula 3 is now a major interest. In Britain, use of the Volkswagen engine is now almost universal among the Formula 3 front-runners.

Meanwhile, the GTI itself was becoming established in rallying. For rally engine preparation Rosorius has used specialists closer to home — firms like Berg, Schrick and even — in the evenings after most of the students have left — the Science Department of Hannover University! In the early days of competition Golfs the academics were pressed into making camshafts for Group 1 engines!

Those first 1,600cc GTI Group 1 engines for rallying produced only 120bhp, but in 1978 VW Motorsport produced a Group 2 version. Still based on the 1,598cc single-cam unit, but taking advantage of the more liberal Group 2 rules to fit a special cylinder head and Zenith fuel injection, this one developed 180bhp. It was when using this engine that Jochi Kleint — a VW Motorsport regular as a result of his rallycross exploits — held second place in the opening stages of the Hunsruck Rally behind the Lancia Stratos of eventual winner Walter Rohrl. Clearly, the rally Golf GTI had some potential.

That was proved the following year, 1979, when Swedish star Per Eklund was persuaded to drive a GTI in the September Sachs-Baltic Rally. It was the car's first major rally win — leading home 154 starters, including two Toyota Celicas driven by Achim Warmbold and Tapio Rainio. VW Motorsport's technical co-ordinator, Andreas Hansch, remembers the occasion with delight. 'We were a little embarrassed to approach such a great driver who we knew did such fantastic things with Saab. We were amazed and delighted when he accepted. We even brought along extra brake pads for him!'

The extra-wide wheelarches show that this is an extensively modified Group 2 car which in 1979 won the Sachs-Baltic Rally outright driven by Saab works driver Per Eklund.

Eklund's achievement in the 1980 Monte Carlo Rally — he held a place in the top three for much of the event and finished fifth overall — was a tremendous encouragement for VW Motorsport's GTI rally programme.

Line-up of stars for the 1980 Sachs Baltic Rally — left to right, Pentti Airikkala, Per Eklund and Jean-Luc Therier all drove GTIs. Eklund and Therier became Volkswagen regulars.

That's the way to do it — Kalle Grundel in full cry in the Mark 1 Group A GTI. He drove the same car to a most impressive eighth place in the Lombard RAC Rally in 1983.

Such was the cordiality of the relationship built up between Eklund and the small team from Hannover that Per agreed to contest the Monte Carlo Rally the following year. In particularly icy and difficult conditions the Swede excelled, and for much of the event he was to amaze his new team by keeping the car in the top three places overall — only dropping to fifth on the final night when better weather conditions and consequent snow and ice-free roads allowed some of his more powerful opponents to overtake him. Later that year both Frenchman Jean-Luc Therier and Finn Pentti Airikkala formed a three-car team for the Sachs-Baltic Rally.

The following year witnessed victory in the German Rally Championship, and development of the Group 4, 16-valve, twin-overhead-camshaft Oettinger cylinder head for rallying — a very different design to that of the recently announced roadgoing engine — which boosted power to 193bhp. In 1982, Eklund was entered in the San Remo World Championship Rally with one of these cars, forcing it into the top 10 before eventually retiring with clutch failure after 43 of the 56 special stages.

And then came Kalle Grundel. Recommended to Andy Hansch by fellow Swedes, and fresh from a remarkable fifth overall — in a self-prepared Golf GTI — on the Swedish Rally the previous year, Kalle was nevertheless treated with

Grundel, right, with 1984 co-driver Peter Diekmann, was an unlikely new star, starting with the VW team in his mid-thirties, but has since gone on to Group B rallying with Peugeot.

The Mark 2 GTI quickly became competitive in Group A rallying and proved easier to drive in rally conditions than the original. This is Franz Wittmann on the 1985 Rally of Portugal.

some initial circumspection by the Germans. After all, at 34, he hardly represented the epitome of a young hot-shoe.

Something of a Sword of Damocles thus hung over Grundel — he had to finish rallies, post consistently good results, yet not go off the road in the process.

Groups 1-4 were replaced by a new international classification with the mass production-based cars in Group A and the rally 'specials', like the Quattro and its four-wheel-drive followers, in Group B. With the arrival of the 1,800cc engine, the Group A GTI could produce around 160bhp. An astonishing performance by Grundel in the 1983 RAC Rally — eighth overall among the world's best rally machinery — showed that the Golf would be a strong Group A contender. Entry in World Rally Championship events was planned for 1984.

The arrival of the Mark 2 Golf halfway through the season clearly improved the team's competitiveness. Grundel confirms that the original GTI was a nervous steed on gravel special stages: 'You had to do a lot of work with the old car, both with the steering wheel and the pedals, just to hold a line through a corner, because it jumped around so much. And you needed experience to drive it really fast because it would spin very easily in bumpy conditions. So you had to have a real feel for the car before this happened, not *as* it happened — by then, it was too late!

'The new car gives you far more warning. It's much more forgiving, so it can be made to go much faster. The longer wheelbase gives it more stability and the suspension has longer travel — those two things make it completely new, and far better.'

In the days of the old car, VW Motorsport had managed to reduce the GTI's weight to comfortably below the minimum class limit of 880kg, with the result that they were actually adding ballast to make the car legal. The newly shaped — and considerably bigger — car was painstakingly assembled to the point where the 1984 RAC Rally vehicle weighed just 886kg.

High-ratio power steering was introduced for the first time on the 1984 Tour de Corse — and not a moment too soon, for Grundel found that he was utterly exhausted, even with power steering fitted, at the end of the longest 50, 60 and 70-kilometre special stages: 'I couldn't even turn the wheel, so without power steering we might just as well have forgotten about the whole thing'. Recently,

Richard Lloyd raced a GTI in the RAC British Saloon Car Championship for several seasons and enjoyed great success in his class. Preparation of his first car brought GTi Engineering into being.

the team have been working on different-ratio power steering for tarmac and gravel surfaces.

Grundel scarcely ever uses the handbrake as part of his competition Golf driving technique, both because he feels that the resulting attitude of the car scrubs off too much speed, and because it's difficult on slick racing tyres to be absolutely precise with the car's final position on the road at the end of the manoeuvre.

Like many of today's rally driving elite,he drives very 'straight', trying always to cling to a racing line, 'because it's obviously quicker, and when you haven't got that much power anyway, going sideways is an indulgence I couldn't afford'.

In 20 consecutive events with the GTI up to the end of 1984 and his departure to Peugeot Germany, Grundel retired just three times, his best results including ninth in the Monte Carlo Rally, eighth in Portugal and sixth in the San Remo — not bad for a Group A car in the World Championship!

The GTI had won its spurs in rallying, where a well-driven nimble car can often make up for a relative lack of horsepower. What of racing, where its success would have to be measured against cars of similar size and power?

In Britain, the GTI's competition career started by chance early in 1977 when racing driver Richard Lloyd noticed a small advertisement in the motoring section of the *Sunday Times* for a silver LHD version — allegedly the first ever GTI to find its way to these shores.

With an unsuccessful Opel Commodore racing season behind him, and a lacklustre catering venture seeming to offer little hope for the future, the astute Lloyd journeyed to the East End of London, bought the car on the spot, and in discovering its widely publicized attributes for himself, decided on one more stab at racing.

The Golf's first races took place with only legal and security requirements

When Lloyd moved on to other things — like a Porsche 956 Group C Le Mans car — several others came into the Tricentrol series with Golf GTIs. This is John Morris' Golf GTI, leading its sister-under-the-skin, a Scirocco GTI.

Volkswagen engines, derived from the GTI but enlarged to 2-litres, became standard wear for winners in Formula 3 racing. Martin Brundle was VW-powered to take second place in the 1983 British F3 series, which led to a Grand Prix drive with Tyrrell.

taken care of — it was mechanically absolutely standard. But Volkswagen UK, as the importers were then known, took immediate interest, and armed with some official backing, Lloyd approached the famous race preparation concern of Broadspeed Engineering, with a view to persuading Ralph Broad's organization to prepare the car.

But this was an unhappy time for Broadspeed. The firm's deal with Jaguar to prepare works XJC models for the European Touring Car Championship was going sour, and employees were leaving with the rapidity which suggested a rapidly foundering vessel.

Brian Ricketts, a Broadspeed employee, was given responsibility for their new client, but after only a handful of races, and despite the fact that the car itself proved excellent in its new competition role, Lloyd, like many others at the time, found himself with telephone number bills.

Ricketts, a highly talented, self-taught, seat-of-the-pants engineer, had no interest in remaining at Broadspeed. Lloyd, for his part, could not afford to keep the car there. A joint venture seemed logical, just as did a choice of venue: Silverstone, a mid-point between Ricketts' home town of Stratford and Lloyd's home in Barnes, West London.

By remortgaging his house, and considerable exercises in the art of begging and borrowing, Lloyd scraped up enough money to launch a new company. It already had one 'client' — Volkswagen UK. Thus, GTi Engineering, and the Golf GTI as a race car, were born in Britain, and engine specialist Ricketts rapidly put the new company on the map with competition preparation work for a number of eager motor racing clients.

As recently as 1983, Alan Minshaw, regular club racer and proprietor of Demon Tweeks, the highly successful Cheshire-based mail order motor accessory business, ran a 1,600cc GTI with great success in the British Saloon

Here's a GTI with 390bhp! The power comes from two Oettinger 16-valve GTI 1.8 engines, one in the conventional position, the other at the rear, with cooling air fed to it through roof ducts. It was built for the Pike's Peak hill-climb in Colorado, USA, where it was driven by Jochi Kleint but beaten by Michele Mouton in the Quattro from VW's associates in Ingolstadt. The Twin Golf is said to be capable of 160mph and go from 0-62mph in 4.6 seconds.

Car Championship — its 160bhp Group A engine with a specification including a 12:1 compression ratio, Cosworth pistons and a Schrick camshaft, all prepared at Silverstone by Ricketts. Andy Dawson, himself a motorsport preparation specialist of some repute, pronounced this car superb — 'an inexpensive, simple-to-maintain and reliable international race car'.

This, in essence, has always been what competing in a GTI is about, since to this day almost all Golfs prepared to international motor sport regulations are virtually standard in terms of suspension mountings and geometry. The only real changes in this area are an increase in negative camber at the front, by enlarged holes in the strut-to-hub carrier mounting bolts and offset top strut mounts.

The German national racing championships have seen a large number of GTIs over the last few years. In Britain the emphasis has switched to rallying following Grundel's 1983 RAC success. The British importers gave their official blessing to Audi for this branch of the sport. Besides, after years of rear-drive Escort domination, Britain had few accomplished front-wheel-drive exponents.

Grundel's Group A win — by a country mile — in the 1983 RAC Rally changed all that. Aspiring rally drivers throughout the country suddenly wanted to drive Golfs. Grundel's works car was rallied in Britain by privateer Chris Lord in 1984 and the belated arrival of the production 16-valve twin-cam engine in mid-1985 promised further interest from rally competitors keen to wrest Group A in the British Championship from Rover and Toyota.

Volkswagen in Britain are fielding a Junior Rally Team in the 1986 British National Rally Championship. Four Group A GTIs are being made available to young drivers from England, Scotland, Wales and Northern Ireland, with the most successful going forward to a works-backed drive in the RAC Rally.

Meanwhile, VW Motorsport have built a *twin-engined* Golf GTI, following previous projects with Jetta and Scirocco. This may be an elaborate way of matching Audi's four-wheel drive — it was built specifically for the Pike's Peak hill-climb in the United States — but it shows that the Hannover department still has ideas aplenty. One, clearly, is a lightweight Group A GTI with 200bhp from a 16-valve engine and the forthcoming Syncro four-wheel drive.

So the GTI's competition career is far from over. What we have seen so far may just be the end of the beginning.

Joining the Golf clubs

Let's face it — we all enjoy talking cars, don't we? Some organizations for GTI owners

A car as admired as the Golf GTI generates a special pride of ownership. For most GTI drivers, the car is more than simply a means of transport. There is a real enthusiasm for it, enhanced by sharing with others of like mind. It's not surprising, then, that there are owners' clubs all around Europe.

In Britain there are over 50 Volkswagen owners' clubs ranging from the general social to the very specific for models such as the Karmann Ghia and the early 'split window' Beetles. The biggest and longest established is the Volkswagen Owners Club (GB) — the only one to be affiliated to the RAC for motor sport organisation. The national VW club, which is totally independent of the factory or importers, has centres all over the country. Local and national events are organised and the VWOC is involved in the annual 'VW Action' gathering — the biggest one-make event in Britain. National facilities include a breakdown aid scheme and discounts on insurance and other services. The national club runs a GTI Register — a kind of club within the club — which ensures that there are GTI classes at concours and other events.

Details of the Volkswagen Owners Club (GB) are available from: Mrs. P. Daniel, 66 Pinewood Green, Iver Heath, Buckinghamshire. Tel: Iver (0753) 651538.

A couple of years ago Michael Kingdon, a GTI driver and the owner of a car valeting business in Nottingham, thought that owners of these most sporting Volkswagens deserved a complete club of their own. So he started one. Since then the GTI Drivers' Club has gone from strength to strength. By mid-1985 it had over 600 members in the UK.

'When I first got my GTI I noticed that there was a tremendous camaraderie between owners — every other GTI I came across gave a flash or its driver a friendly wave,' Michael remembers. That shared enthusiasm is now organised at some kind of event every few weeks from purely social weekends in a nice hotel to exhibitions, talks and concours. For the last two years the club has run a special track test session at Goodwood, which has given GTI owners the chance to explore the limits of their cars in the safety of a closed circuit.

The GTI Drivers' Club is also completely independent and offers a range of club regalia and GTI equipment including sweaters, jackets and number plates with the club motif and car parts such as Mintex and Tar-Ox brake pads for the Mark 1.

For more information contact chairman Michael Kingdon at 17 Hereford

GTI companionship — the parade round the WortherSee during the 1985 GTI Treffen. 1,160 cars attended.

Road, Gedling, Nottingham NG4 4WF. Tel: Nottingham (0602) 780064.

The biggest annual get-together of GTIs — perhaps the largest gathering of one type of car in the world — is held each summer in Austria. It started simply enough as a *treffen* (convention) for GTI owners in the village of Maria Worth on the edge of WortherSee, a lake in southern Austria. After a successful small-scale meeting in 1982, Volkswagen encouraged a repeat by circulating details to GTI owners in Germany and Austria. Nearly 800 cars turned up in 1983.

It had become too big for the local organisation, so Volkswagen, in association with the local tourist board, stepped in. In 1984 over 1,000 GTIs attended and in 1985 there were no less than 1,160 and over 3,000 people at the four day party which was opened by the most famous Austrian GTI driver, World Champion Niki Lauda.

The GTI Treffen consists of exhibitions, talks and film shows, 'treasure hunt' rallies and driving slaloms, but mostly it is giant get-together which has now expanded to the neighbouring town. Highspot of the 1985 event, attended by GTI owners from seven countries, was a parade of all the cars present around the lake — a six-mile GTI traffic jam!

VAG Audi VW BLUE RIBAND

DEALER OF EXCELLENCE 1985/4

Vic Lee, Sales Manager, Whitehouse Bexley, is seen here driving his VW Golf GTi to Victory at Brands Hatch during the Monroe production Saloon car championship — his fifth victory this year. Proof that there's not much that we don't know about performance hatchbacks — and there is still no competition for the GTi.

The VW Golf GTi — still no1 hatchback

If you would like to test drive an ultimate hatchback — phone Vic Lee now. You won't be disappointed.

Whitehouse

Blendon Road, Bexley, Kent **Tel: 01-301 3050**